MODE *series directed by Maria Luisa Frisa*

–1– Alessandra Vaccari
  WIG-WAG. THE FLAGS OF FASHION

–2– Antonio Mancinelli
  ANTONIO MARRAS

–3– Claudio Marenco Mores
  FROM FIORUCCI TO THE GUERRILLA STORE

–4– Vittoria Caterina Caratozzolo
  IRENE BRIN. ITALIAN STYLE IN FASHION

–5– James Sherwood
  THE LONDON CUT. SAVILE ROW. BESPOKE TAILORING

–6– Paola Colaiacomo
  FACTIOUS ELEGANCE. PASOLINI AND THE MALE FASHION

–7– Vittoria Caterina Caratozzolo - Judith Clark - Maria Luisa Frisa
  SIMONETTA. THE FIRST LADY OF ITALIAN FASHION

–8– Elda Danese
  THE HOUSE DRESS. A STORY OF EROTICISM AND FASHION

–9– Olivier Saillar, Oliviero Toscani
  WORKWEAR. WORK FASHION SEDUCTION

Gianfranco Ferré
Lessons in Fashion

edited by Maria Luisa Frisa

Marsilio MODE FONDAZIONE PITTI DISCOVERY

Special thanks to
Gian Paolo Barbieri, Herb Ritts Foundation, Tyen

translation
Huw Evans

photographs of shows
Alfredo Albertone
Piero Biasion
Aldo Castoldi
Leonardo Cendamo
Graziano Ferrari
Karim
Stefano Pandini
Ignazio Parravicini
Nicola Ranaldi
Bruno Rinaldi
Dino Scrimali
Graziella Vigo
M. Cristina Vimercati

cover
Gianfranco Ferré Prêt-à-porter, S/S 1993,
black felt-tip pen and black and red wax pastel on cardboard
inside cover
Gianfranco Ferré Prêt-à-porter, A/W 1982-1983
Pencil, black India ink felt-tip pen, red, royal blue
and yellow felt-tip pens on cardboard
inside back cover
Gianfranco Ferré Prêt-à-porter, S/S 1982
Pencil, black India ink felt-tip pen, yellow, green, red, turquoise,
blue and black wax pastels and applications of silver foil on paper
back cover
Gianfranco Ferré Prêt-à-porter, S/S 1993
black felt-tip pen on paper

The volume has been produced in collaboration with

Fondazione Gianfranco Ferré

© 2009 by Fondazione Pitti Discovery - www.pittimmagine.com

© 2009 by Fondazione Gianfranco Ferré - www.fondazionegianfrancoferre.com

© 2009 by Marsilio Editori® s.p.a. in Venezia - www.marsilioeditori.it

first edition October 2009 - ISBN 88-317-9974
No part of this publication may be produced, stored in a retrieval system, or transmitted in any form
or by any means without the prior permission in writing of the copyright holder and the publisher

Printed by Grafiche Nardin, Ca' Savio - Cavallino - Treporti (Venezia)
for Marsilio Editori® s.p.a. in Venezia

Contents

6   Foreword
Rita Airaghi

11   Lessons in fashion
Maria Luisa Frisa

19   Design in Fashion

27   Créateur/couturier

43   Composition and Fashion

65   Men's Fashion

73   Jewerly between East and West,
a Balancing of Design and Fantasy

87   Designing the Material

110   Fashion Design and Creativity
Facing the Challenges of the New Millennium

119   Creativity and Working Method

133   The Tailor of Two Cities

141   Exotic Inspirations

153   The Forms of Emotion. Giving Form to Feelings

162   Biography

164   Essential Bibliography

Foreword
Rita Airaghi *Director of the Fondazione Gianfranco Ferré*

The Fondazione Gianfranco Ferré was set up in 2008 with a mission that is at once simple and complex: to index, preserve and make available to the public the immense quantity of materials–clothes, drawings, photographs, texts, film strips and much more–some of it already organized, the rest scattered and muddled, in order to document the work of one of the most important figures in Italian fashion. The foundation also has the objective of promoting projects and carrying out activities that do not just follow in the wake of Gianfranco Ferré's ideas and poetics, reappraising his conception of fashion, aesthetics and the culture of design, but make the archive itself a lively place of research and source of ideas, and thus not limited to the mere organization and conservation of the materials in a vision frozen in time.

Gianfranco Ferré's archive is undoubtedly exceptional in the quality and quantity of its contents, and offers students and creative people the possibility to reconstruct all the phases of his design and method of working, investigating their dynamics and results.

Fashion archives do not solely have to meet the need of imposing order so as to preserve information, but also and above all answer to the logic of the fragmentation of the past and its creative recomposition. The archive is a place in which the traces of the past can be examined in their fragmentary state, and are thus capable of triggering new relationships and new chains of invention. Adopting this approach, the Fondazione Gianfranco Ferré favors a view of the fashion archive as a means of bringing memory to life. A way of liberating the fragments of the past and generating an "aura" around these traces. And of putting them back into circulation, rather than fixing them in a collection of materials to be catalogued.

This is the aim of the foundation's first project, the publication of the book Lessons in Fashion with a selection of Ferré's lectures and talks, given on a regular basis from the nineties and preserved in the archive.

Gianfranco Ferré had always devoted himself with conviction and commitment to what was for him an inescapable duty: placing his own experience at the disposal of all those who wanted to learn the craft of fashion or investigate the dynamics of creative practices. These lectures bear witness to that commitment: the last, given at Milan Polytechnic only three days before he died, but also his teaching at the Domus Academy in the eighties and during his presidency of the Accademia di Brera.

Recognizing the importance of training, the foundation has already made awards for outstanding graduate theses in order to help new talents to pursue their dreams and their passions and to promote Italian schools of fashion and their efforts to bring creative people to maturity.

After this book will come others, just as there will be other projects, always with a view to the sharing and critical interpretation of the archive.

The Fondazione Gianfranco Ferré wants to be a lively place of research and exchange, open to all and capable of putting itself on the line with projects that, through the retrieval and reexamination of the materials in the archive, are able to confront and support fashion in the present.

Gianfranco Ferré
Lessons in Fashion

Lessons in fashion
Maria Luisa Frisa

Design for an installation of crinoline in the Medici Chapels, *First Fashion Biennale*, Florence 1996
mixed media: b/w photocopy overlaid with a b/w print from a negative onto which original drawings made with white lacquer (correction fluid) on tracing paper have also been superimposed

Many will have been perplexed by the parallel I draw between architecture and tailoring.
(Adolf Loos)

It is not a precise article of clothing which I think about, but details, attitudes, a way of moving, ideas in movement.
(Gianfranco Ferré)

We present here a series of lectures given by Gianfranco Ferré over a span of time stretching from 1994 to 2007. The last of them was given on June 14, 2007, just a few days before he died. The lectures have been put together by Rita Airaghi, Ferré's first and highly valued assistant and now president of the Fondazione Gianfranco Ferré, who is imparting order, form and visibility to an archive of extraordinary importance to the history of Italian fashion. The backdrop to these lectures is the world: in fact they were given in locations ranging from London to Tokyo and from Milan to Istanbul, passing through Shanghai, Turin and Florence. The audience was different on each occasion: students at Milan Polytechnic or Central Saint Martin's College in London; the elite of the fashion world, as for the one given in Istanbul at one of the Luxury Conferences coordinated by Suzy Menkes for *The International Herald Tribune*; or again participants in the International Textile Forum organized by the Fondazione Ratti at the Villa d'Este in Cernobbio. The lectures (with one exception) were accompanied by many slides ?that are reproduced here? and that can be seen as telling a story in their own right. And they record, in the words and reflections of the designer, not just his poetics and his way of working and relating to fashion, but also his own story, a fundamental piece in the history of that Made in Italy, of that Italian vision of fashion which imposed itself so forcefully on the world from the end of the seventies onward. In these texts we find his obsessions and his themes, as well as the close relationship between fashion and architecture, starting from the centrality of the body as a first and fundamental referent around which the construction of the garment turns. The three-dimensionality that unites the two disciplines. And of course his approach to design that led him to apply the same balance of form to fashion. Or again the inspiration that came above all from his journeys to the East, from his curiosity, from the attention he paid to everything in a mix of past and future, East and West, reality and fantasy from which Ferré drew dreams, visions and emotions. The importance of the colors and materials, continually put to the test through the use of technology to create unheard-of combinations. And then what it meant to him to design for women, to design for men. But also the clear awareness that fashion is a globalized project of communication and that the fashion designer is the guarantor of the creative process at all levels. "If I look at the origins of my creativity, I discover that what I put into effect every day is a mode of operation that can boast ancient roots: a 'humanistic' attitude that finds its expressive force in the cult of quality and beauty, in the sense of tradition, in the love of harmony and balance. My creativity takes on concrete form in the daily confrontation with forms, colors and materials: it is an exercise in rigor and determination; it is the continual desire to innovate and experiment."

With hindsight, we can see just how pioneering was his pressing need to explain his work in order to share and hand on a know-how of fashion: a sharing whose necessity and urgency had not yet really been grasped in Italy. For Ferré the passing down of his knowledge, his experience and his skill was almost a moral obligation. He had no sense of jealousy or mistrust. So he had no reservations about getting involved when he was invited to be one of the group of people who founded the Domus Academy in Milan, a school that was born out of the multitude of requests that had arrived at the magazine *Domus*–edited since the beginning of the eighties by Alessandro Mendini–from students and architects all over the world who wanted to learn design in Italy, in the country that after the revolution carried out by radical groups like Archizoom or Superstudio was now considered the discipline's new homeland. The architect of fashion, to use the label with which he was most often defined by the world's press, became the director of the fashion department, which he ran for seven years from 1982, right up until the time when he accepted the great challenge of becoming creative director of the Maison Christian Dior (the first Italian designer to be called on to play such a role in France). He realized with regret that it would have been impossible, in that "creative–as well as physical and geographic–commuting between Milan and Paris" (*The Tailor of Two Cities* would be the title, derived from the epithet applied to him by an American journalist, of a lecture he gave in 2003), to go on teaching and supervising the department with the same commitment he had lavished on it up until then and decided to leave the school.

It is very interesting to read, one after the other, the lectures that are being published here for the first time, practically in their original version in order to preserve and convey the immediacy and freshness of a text conceived to be read in public or used as an outline. They are lectures that, starting out each time from a particular theme, offer endless lessons and insights into Ferré's method as well as practice of design: "[...] an aptitude for design that is founded on the conception of the garment as the result of a planned and conscious intervention in forms. An elaboration of simple, elementary forms that leads to intentionally complex and intricate results. A process of construction that starts out from a two-dimensional reality–that of the design traced on paper in the form of a drawing–but with the human body as an indispensable referent from the very beginning. The human body as a three-dimensional entity *par excellence*, with its physicality, its real requirements of movement, its dynamics of relationship with what covers it and with the surrounding environment," he explained to students at Milan Polytechnic on March 14, 1997. In these words it seems possible to hear an echo of the experience he had had at the Florence Biennale the previous year, when the designer had emerged victorious from a confrontation with the beauty, but also with the power of an extraordinary work of architecture of the past. All it takes is a photograph of pieces of colored marble, precious materials worked by skilled craftsmen of the past, to give vivid form to the vision of the Medici Chapels visited by Ferré. Clothes, or perhaps it would be better to say marvelous and beautiful designs hung in the air squeezed into the space beneath the historic dome. "The crinoline of the 20th century: this is what makes some of the garments I have chosen to include in my project unique. It is light, almost airy, to the point where it made me think of hanging it up to fill the sublime volumes of the Medici Chapels with its richness, visible in its perfection under the sumptuous hems of a dress, lifted by an imaginary gust of wind [...]." An interpretation of volumes and space that leads us to his white blouse. To the perfect interpretation, always handled in new and extraordinary ways, breaking up the volumes and reassembling them in acrobatic forms that are capable of having the solidity of a work of architecture, of the "piece, almost *par excellence*, of a freely chosen wardrobe." "It swells and lifts with movement, as if gravity were absent. It rises like a corolla to frame the face. It sculpts the body to turn it into a second skin. It is the versatile interpreter of the most varied material qualities: of impalpable organza, of crisp taffeta, of shiny satin, of duchesse, poplin, georgette, chiffon [...]."

The paradox of fashion is exactly the same as that of architecture. Apparently the space precedes us, but it is our occupation of it that makes us perceive it. The movement of cognition is from the inside to the outside: living in space means making it to our measure and being made to its measure. Like the house, the first unit of space, clothing is habitation and habit.

In these texts Ferré talks about his creative practices. As an architect, he knows very well what it means to give form to an idea, to an intuition: "We should keep an eye on Ferré, for he is an architect. He came to the profession when it was well defined, he interprets it with awareness," wrote Silvia Giacomoni in 1984. In fact Ferré had taken a degree in architecture under a teacher like Franco Albini with a thesis whose title appears already to be a declaration of his future intentions, *Methodology of the Approach to Composition*. And his first collaborations were with designers like Walter Albini and Christiane Bailly, who marked a turning point in the birth of ready-to-wear.

Ferré knew what it meant to draw, to outline a sketch on paper and turn it into a technical drawing, prelude of the paper pattern, two-dimensional relative of the architectural model, which in the rigor of its measurements and proportions, transforms materials and colors into an object of fashion. The need to question himself about his way of designing a garment and a collection, of passing from an intuition, from an image, to a fascinating form that could be replicated in the numbers and the lead times required for distribution, was certainly in the first place a reflection of a personal desire to define the meaning of his own profession in an ever clearer way: "It is necessary to have an inner formula, a way of expressing yourself, of analyzing," he wrote in his now unfortunately unobtainable *A un giovane stilista*. A small book, published first in French as *Lettres à un jeune couturier* in 1995 and the following year in Italian, in which he responds to the letters/questions of Federico, a young man impatient to discover "the little world of fashion" that Ferré in the first of his responses prefers to define as "the little theater of fashion," in order to become a fashion designer. "It is true that I became interested in fashion only after much head-scratching. Sometimes I am asked why I gave up architecture. Simply because, at the end of the sixties, everyone in Milan had been caught up in the fever for design. Except me. I don't see any difference between the architecture of a building and that of an item of clothing. You have to go along with the creative intuition that dictates your sensibility, then organize it methodically and bring it to the final result."

But this readiness to expose himself, notwithstanding his shyness, is also part–as his personal involvement in the Domus Academy, the lectures published in this book and the *Lettres* demonstrate–of that sense of responsibility, of that profound and sincere consciousness, without any desire for self-promotion, of the obligations that each of us has toward others, of the great value that generosity can have in passing on one's own experience. In an ethical–and very Lombard–perspective that required him to make what he had had the fortune to learn and receive available to all, for the common good. On the value of education, of study: "My studies have taught me a discipline, a way of thinking about and seeing things. The ability to analyze the mechanisms of research, in order to establish a connection between the various impressions and their applications in a specific context." This is why he chose to help the young to direct and cultivate their own talent so as to give form and concrete expression to their dreams and passions.

Gianfranco Ferré was the only designer on the Italian fashion scene who felt this need to involve himself in the training of the next generation of creative people. Part of the reason for this undoubtedly lay in the fact that he had attended a school like that of architecture, with teachers like Franco Albini who combined the practice of design with education as a further opportunity for creativity and exchange.

"First of all you must realize that no one enters the world of fashion by chance. It is a choice and, just as in the theater, it is always necessary to take account of what the critics teach us and, starting from there, to reflect. It goes without saying that we should not forget to be self-critical [...]. We have to learn to shape our discipline. In order not to be victims of fashion and its little world, we must be ourselves. I would add that is better to remain in the wings, instead of always being in the spotlight on stage," Gianfranco Ferré wrote to Federico at the very beginning of the book, making it clear that fashion goes well beyond the superficial interpretation with which it is often dismissed. Fashion speaks of us, of our time. Styles change rapidly and allow us to look back into the past and forward into the future. Fashion performs many social, aesthetic and psychological functions: it binds them together and is able to express them all at once. Diana Vreeland once said that "fashion is the avant-garde of circumstance," for it is truly difficult to draw a line between clothing and body and between life and dress.

SOURCES IN THE TEXT
Judith Clark, "Installing Allusions," in *The Art of Fashion. Installing Allusions.* Rotterdam 2009.
Paola Colaiacomo and Vittoria Caterina Caratozzolo, *Cartamodello, Antologia di scrittori e scritture sulla moda.* Rome 2000.
Gianfranco Ferré, *A un giovane stilista.* Milan 1996.
Giusi Ferré, *Gianfranco Ferré.* Milan 1988.
Silvia Giacomoni, *L'Italia della moda.* Milan 1984.
Wu Ming, *New Italian Epic. Letteratura, sguardo obliquo, ritorno al futuro.* Turin 2009.
Luigi Settembrini and Franca Sozzani, *Visitors.* Milan 1996.
Elisabeth Wilson, *Adorned in Dreams. Fashion and Modernity.* London 1985.bbi:

Turin, April 22, 1996
Design in Fashion
Second international forum on automobile styling
Architettura e tipologia dell'auto del 2000

1.
Gianfranco Ferré
Prêt-à-Porter,
F/W 1992-93

There are several distinctive characteristics that make fashion design different from other sectors of design. I'm referring first of all to the more recent development of fashion–and Italian fashion in particular–in the light of its international success and its leading role in the world.

In the first place it is necessary to take note of the fact that design can be considered a new discipline–not having been around even for a century yet–and one that is continually evolving. In particular, design in fashion has only been a reality for a very few decades, that is to say since fashion became an industrial phenomenon to all intents and purposes: mass consumption, mass production, distribution all over the world and the consequent necessity for planning, quality control, comparison of prices. Drawing directly on my personal experience, however, I have to point out that, alongside factory-made fashion–so-called *prêt-à-porter*–there is the sector of *haute couture*, high fashion with its exceptional expressive possibilities: a world in which everything is made by hand and to measure, where stylistic experiments and solutions inconceivable in *prêt-à-porter* are possible. In Christian Dior's atelier I had the unique opportunity to operate in an authentic and extraordinary artisan workshop, a laboratory for the creation of prototypes, of one-off pieces in which I could try out structural and material ideas that were sometimes then transferred into *prêt-à-porter*.

In this sense, *haute couture* can be thought of as the Formula One of fashion. Yet the fashion phenomenon that has most influenced and characterized the evolution of patterns of behavior and daily life over the last few decades, partly due to its truly universal dissemination, is factory-made *prêt-à-porter*. A dimension in which a fundamental role is played by the designer, or rather the fashion designer, who has to be able to mediate between creativity and aspects of production, between imagination and market realities.

So what are the distinctive characteristics of industrial design in fashion? In the first place we can speak of continuous design, in the sense that the input of creativity extends without a break, garment after garment, collection after collection. It might be thought that fashion is in fact engaged in wholly superficial modifications, frivolous and of no substance: something that is the complete opposite of the basic principle of industrial design, which aims instead at the creation of definitive objects. It is not like that: the continual process of design in fashion is

2.
Dior Couture,
F/W 1994-95

3.
Dior Couture,
F/W 1993-94

4.
Dior Couture,
S/S 1995

5.
Dior Couture,
F/W 1994-95

to some extent reminiscent of artistic research, for example that of the painter who goes on evolving from work to work, with results that are different each time but have the coherence of a personal and individual style.

Another characteristic of design applied to fashion becomes clear when we realize that the aim of that design is not the object–the item of clothing–as such, but to have an effect, through the clothing, on the behavior and the taste of individuals. In a world saturated with objects, the fashion designer has to design, or strive to design, the desires of men and women.

From here we move on to another aspect of fashion design, and one that is fundamental today. An aspect that began to emerge about ten or fifteen years ago and that seemed revolutionary with respect to the previous concept of fashion (still considered valid by many). For over ten years, in fact, at the level of the world's trendsetters, it has been possible to speak of

"styles" in fashion. The most important interpreters of style, the ones who guide its evolution, offer men and women a range, a choice of "parallel styles," all "in fashion" but all different. For some years I too have found myself working on two different styles, on two different approaches to identity: that of Gianfranco Ferré and that of Christian Dior, a worldwide symbol of luxury that I have set out to renew in its spirit and in its expressions of elegance.

The activity of the fashion designer who proposes styles of an aesthetic character, and thus styles of behavior as well, presupposes a complex kind of design that cannot be limited to the product. Instead it has to involve all the phases and means of communication and the relationship with the end users. The designer, like the conductor of an orchestra, has to propose and keep under control "the interpretation of the score of style," which also means taking into consideration, among other things, the essential aspects of distribution of product and image. Hence the design of style develops into an authentic global message, characterized by a strong coherence of sensibility.

Fashion is expressed today by styles. And the styles have to evolve, following or anticipating the changes in society, proposing new desires and keeping in touch with new and emerging sensitivities.

In this sense, my design work and the intentions of my research have evolved in two main directions. In the first place I have wanted to intervene in forms, aiming at a simplicity that would leave today's woman–and of course man too–free to add the decorative elements that she prefers, on the basis of her mood, her culture, the nature of the moment. In my recent collections I have made a determined effort to separate the decoration from the essentiality of the lines, aiming at a cleanness of design that leaves room for a personalized aesthetic vocabulary.

In parallel, the quest for clean lines, the conscious move away from decoration, has opened the way for a further field of development: the innovative approach to material. Without doubt, research applied to

6.
Gianfranco Ferré
Prêt-à-Porter,
F/W 1993-94

7.
Gianfranco Ferré
Prêt-à-Porter,
F/W 1996-97

textiles represents the true frontier of fashion in the 21st century, the area in which the changes can be most marked and perceptible. Fashion and creativity are acquiring unprecedented possibilities thanks to the technologies that allow different fibers, natural and synthetic, to be mixed and combined, with each one utilized for its most significant characteristics and potentialities. This is a very interesting aspect: after having explored and revived "forms" and "decorations" derived from all the past ages of our culture and from nonwestern traditions, I believe that today the fashion world has begun to "think" in a positive way, to look ahead to the new millennium.

From this perspective our fashion–Made in Italy–find itself in a favorable position, as it can count on the whole range of extraordinary abilities offered by our manufacturing system. Focused by tradition and by constitution on the activity of processing, our industry–and the textile industry in particular–is able to make the most of its familiarity with experimentation, its quickness in adopting innovative ideas and making them its own, especially in the field of the processing and treatment of material. The new materials, the new mixes, are displaying properties of elasticity and comfort and presenting a look and a feel that were unimaginable hitherto.

The unprecedented possibilities that the material offers to the fashion of our own day are also leading to new solutions of form. Thus technical research becomes "formal" too, since today's materials permit the design of clothing with new forms and new fits that have never been achieved before except at the expense of comfort. And it is precisely comfort that has become the real and concrete goal, the objective of the fashion designer's efforts. An idea of comfort that in fact concerns all the functions of clothing: in physical terms a correspondence between what is worn and the natural forms of the body; in emotional and psychological terms a correspondence between what you wear and your own mental references, your taste, personality and desires.

New York, September 6, 1996
Créateur/couturier
Fashion Institute of Technology

1.
Dior Couture,
F/W 1996-97

I believe the most significant and useful contribution I can offer to an audience of young people who will be working in fashion in the future must start out from a consideration of how creativity, inspiration and imagination find their expression in this field through an extraordinary range of channels and means.

We all know that fashion, a mirror and interpretation of reality, is in fact a phenomenon with a thousand facets, constantly in progress and more fluid than ever today. It is a phenomenon that arises out of individual sensibilities, out of an always personal and subjective interpretation of life and its evolution. A phenomenon that nevertheless appears to be organized into grand common tendencies, operating at different levels, with different reactions from the public and different choices of content.

My analysis is necessarily based on my own experience, accumulated over a career of more than twenty years. An experience that fortunately comprises a fairly wide variety of creative spheres and that commenced, at the end of the sixties, with accessories and jewelry. I soon moved on to factory-made *prêt-à-porter*, for women and men, but without abandoning the design of "objects"–bags, sunglasses, leather goods, perfume bottles. Later came the adventure of high fashion.

Taking advantage of the precision of a certain French terminology to outline my "fields of action," I can make use of the terms of *créateur*–a person who creates collections of *prêt-à-porter* (it should be borne in mind, however, that not all ready-to-wear can be regarded in the strict sense as fruit of the *créateur*'s individual talent, as the reality of production in some countries, such as the United States or Germany, is defined by a more industrial approach)–and *couturier*–the person who designs collections of high fashion.

I have been extremely lucky, and privileged, to have had the opportunity to express myself in both these dimensions. In the first place this has meant being able to make use of different approaches, with their specific codes and rules, to give life and form to an idea, to give concrete expression to my own imagination in a item of clothing or an object.

It has meant being able to benefit from the different experiences and skills that have been accumulated over the decades in both sectors, endowing each of them with autonomous potentialities and opportunities of production. It has meant, finally, establishing different relationships with the real end user of the clothing–the customer of *haute couture*, the customer, man or woman, of *prêt-à-porter*–with a consequent identification of the target for the product and the image.

The position from which I start out, the attitude through which the inspiration, the idea that can emerge in front of something beautiful and exciting, takes its very first steps toward the goal, is independent of the subsequent routes of realization. What brings me to express my idea of elegance, in ready-to-wear as well as high fashion, is an attitude that finds its strength in devotion to quality and beauty, in love of harmony and equilibrium. It is more a state of mind than a professional attitude, belongs more to my mode of being than my mode of working. And, always, the need to "fix" the first impression leads me to draw a quick sketch, a few succinct lines, a silhouette jotted down in its essential points–the shoulders, the waist, the legs stretched out on the sheet of paper–and comprised within diagonals and parallels. Just a few lines, but already a figure: not a garment draped motionless on the hanger, but a living item of clothing with the animation bestowed on it by stride and movement. In the phase that comes immediately afterward the lines

2.
Gianfranco Ferré
Prêt-à-porter
A/W 1991-1992
pencil and wax
pastel on white
cardboard

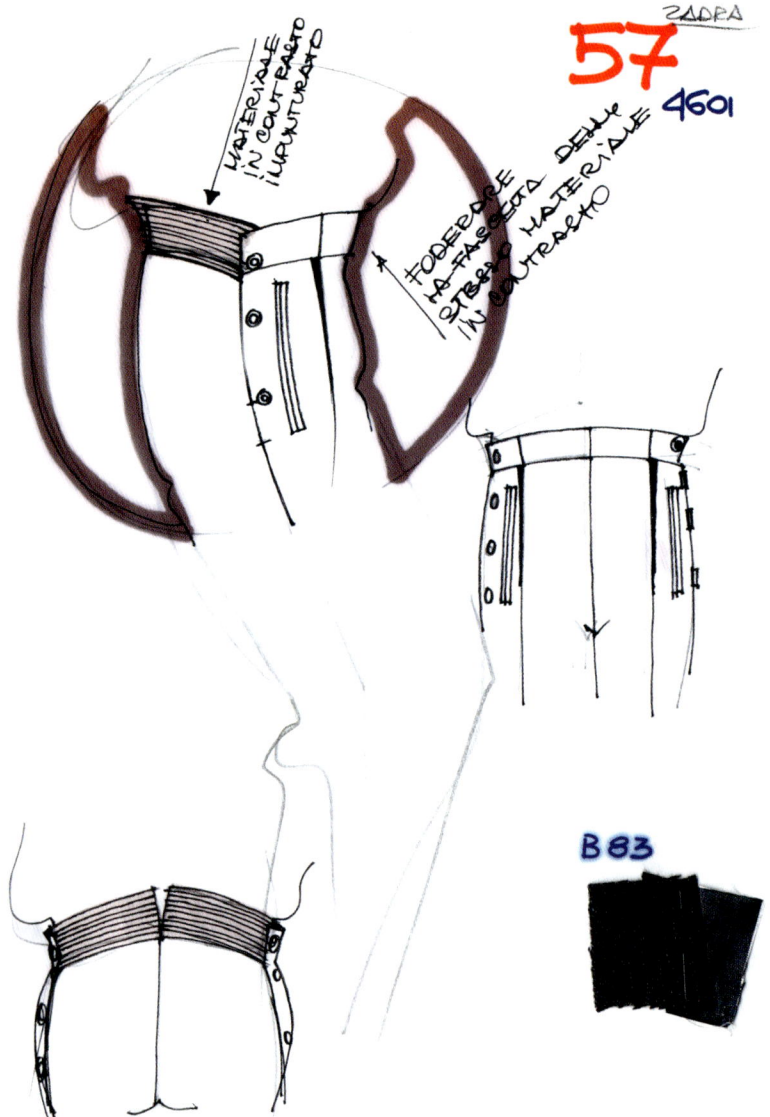

3.
Gianfranco Ferré
Prêt-à-porter
A/W 1983-1984
pencil, black India
ink felt-tip pen and
brown felt-tip pen
on paper

4.
Gianfranco Ferré
Prêt-à-porter A/W
1983-1984
pencil and brown
felt-tip pen on paper

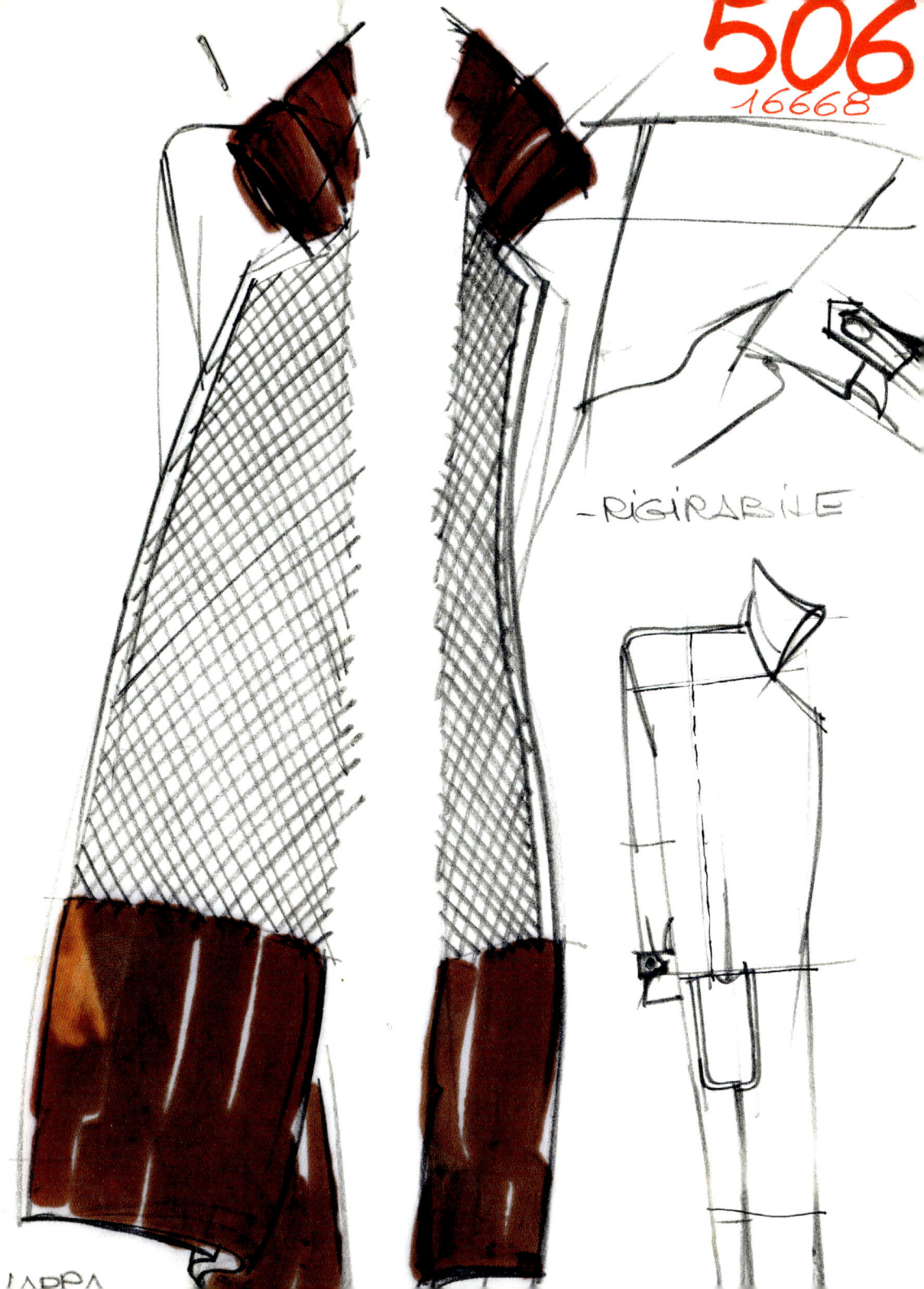

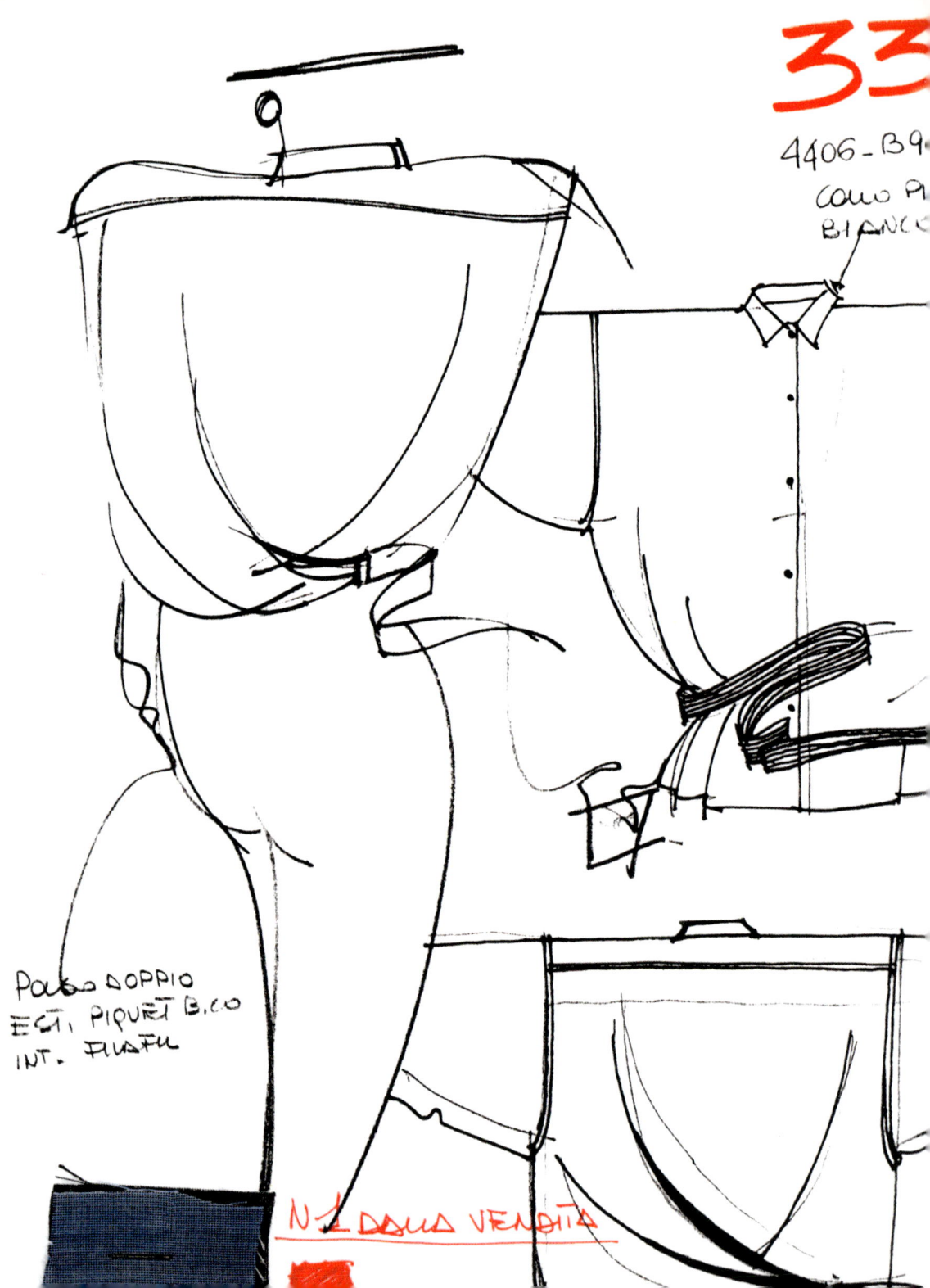

5.
Gianfranco Ferré
Prêt-à-porter
A/W 1983-1984
black India ink felt-tip pen on paper

6.
Gianfranco Ferré
Prêt-à-porter A/W
1988-1989
black India ink felt-tip pen on paper

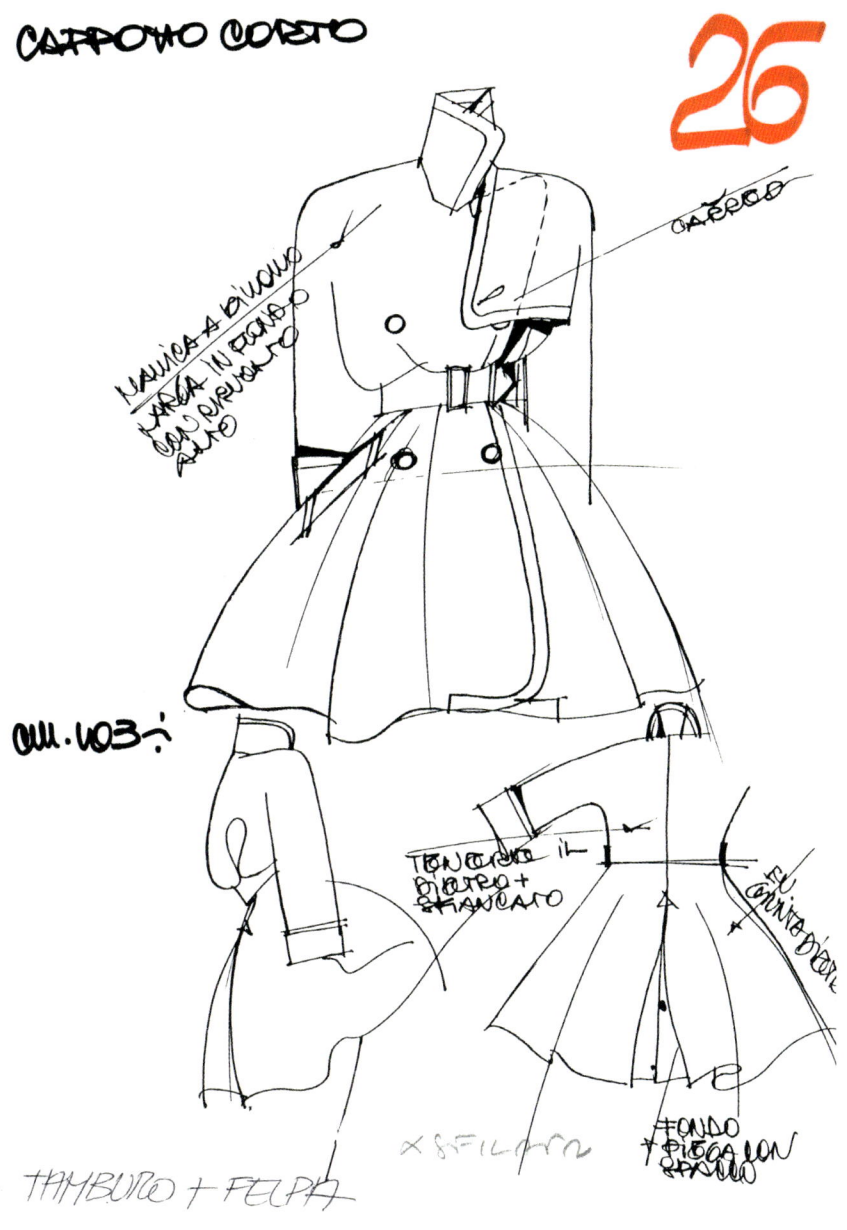

are developed according to the principles of geometry into a technical drawing, in which the forms and details of the clothing are analyzed in elementary terms, the measurements and proportions take on definite outlines, so that the whole thing can be understood by whoever it is, in the company's pattern-making department or the couturier's atelier, that is going to make the first prototype. Out of conviction and training, I'm inclined never to forget that the garment, despite originating in the drawing as a flat shape, is going to cover the body. It exists as a three-dimensional entity. Its form has a function and a meaning chiefly in its relationship with the human figure and in the interpretations of that figure that it offers. As a functional object, the garment comes alive because it is subjected to changes by the person who wears it. It adapts to the body, giving it values and taking them from it. One of the absolute values of dressing today is comfort, freedom of movement, natural wearability. It is no longer possible for clothing to be experienced as an encumbrance, as constriction, to the detriment of the requirements of dynamism and immediacy that are undoubtedly part of life today. Respect for and consideration of these needs represent an axiom, independently of the type of clothing I create, its function or the context in which it will be worn. It might be an evening gown or a svelte pair of pants for daytime wear, a bathing costume or a tailored suit: if I want to create something that has a modern sense and a possibility of concrete use, I have to guarantee an easy and natural wearability. In the role of *créateur* as well as *couturier*, my intervention in the structures of the clothing and my effort to bring out the qualities of the materials are always carried out bearing comfort in mind.

Stopping for a moment to look at an aspect shared by the two worlds in which I have gained my experience, I would like to define the relationship between my creativity and its raw materials: fabrics and colors. In *prêt-à-porter* as in *haute couture* I approach them with an experimental attitude, starting out from a sensation, from the effect I want to obtain. A particular degree of softness, a particular shade of

7.
Dior Couture,
F/W 1996-97

8.
Dior Couture,
F/W 1996-97

color are elements that right from the first design sketch appear to me inseparable from the idea of the garment, from its form and nature. The fabric and color have to be intentional, they have to already be part of the idea at the moment in which it is born.

The end result is reached through attempts, trials and sometimes complicated treatments, in a process that brings the dream–the desired effect–closer to reality. However, it is easy to see that there are concrete and significant differences between the use of fabrics and colors in ready-to-wear and in high fashion. This observation leads us to take a closer look at what differentiates the two levels, especially with regard to the means and methods by which creativity is expressed. It is the methods and means that explain how different the aims are.

With its haughty sense of uniqueness, with its quest for splendor, high fashion represents a special style of dress for special women, which brings with it, always, an aura of exceptionality. The high-fashion

garment, created exclusively for just one woman, is the result of a work process that would not even be conceivable without considering the whole range of abilities on which the atelier can call. The sartorial approach to the work, to the making of the garment, based essentially on manual techniques, and the absolute care taken over detail are the extraordinary means that only the *couturier* has at his disposal and that multiply the possibilities for expression of his creativity. He makes use of them when he determines the structure of the garment, through cuts, seams and other devices studied to measure for each item of clothing; when he chooses the material and the color without any constraint apart from that of the perfect match between desired effect and result; when, to decorate the garment, he can rely on precious handmade embroidery and the whole range of artisan specialties offered him by lace, trimmings, feathers, ribbons and buttons. *Haute couture* is the training ground on which his talent can be put to the harshest test; it is the dimension in which it is possible to make almost any dream come true. Like the picture painted by an artist, every garment is a one-off, against which the techniques, abilities and resources acquired by tradition are checked and applied each time on the basis of specific and absolutely real needs.
The horizons within which the imagination of the *créateur* of *prêt-à-porter* moves are instead those of industrial production and therefore serial reproducibility. Naturally we are talking of a high-level product, whose hallmark continues to be, like the exclusive high-fashion garment, the highest quality. Far from being a fleeting phenomenon, an excess of the eighties, the *créateur* of *prêt-à-porter* represents an element of continuity and success, located as he is in a key position, for he intervenes not just in the type of product, but also in the quality which he vouches for at all levels of the manufacturing process. My label has grown slowly but continually, supported by structures that have permitted the parallel development of my dual role, fashion designer on the one hand and entrepreneur of the brand on the other. A role absolutely dependent on a coupling that–since then–has become inseparable and mutually

beneficial: industry and fashion design. The positive effect of fashion design on industry is that of oiling brains, strategies and mechanisms and pushing them in the direction of research, new technologies and a completeness and efficiency of services so as to render the enterprise not a tool of but a contributor to the new canons of fashion design.

We cannot ignore the fact, however, that the alliance between fashion designer and industry has not always been handled in the right way: when the fashion designer is obliged to play the role of commercial entrepreneur too, then he must also devote his attention to the distribution of his product, while remaining the guarantor of its image and content. In some cases this new and tempting condition has got out of hand and has ended up creating an opposite phenomenon which, in the long run, has proved harmful, for it has created confusion in the market and led to the repetition of products–which I like to call substitutes of the original lines–generating disorientation and taking away the gloss and guarantee that the fashion label has to offer to be credible. By this I am not trying to say that the fashion label should not produce other lines or license them out, but that the basic mistake in many cases has been to offer identical contents to the first line in subsequent ones.

I remember that on its appearance my label was immediately dismissed as too expensive, certainly rich and impressive in its overall image, but still the most costly. While at the beginning all this was regarded as a shortcoming or at least a phenomenon that needed to be explained, after two or three years it became a strength, a reality: this is why my label still exists, unblemished in my view, even though like others I do other things, design other lines, erroneously called "second lines." In its typology and quality my *prêt-à-porter* line is in no way tainted by the product of other lines that have a different content, yet it still has the same underlying image: this permits a greater diffusion of a certain kind of taste, the one that belongs to the Ferré product.

The most serious mistake is to expect a company to improvise the manufacture of different types of product from the ones for which it is structured, in a process of unification. On the birth of my label I decided to make the *prêt-à-porter* collection up out of four individual and distinct sections, each with its own character (clothes, knitwear, leather and swimwear), each manufactured by a leading industry in the sector or at least a company we considered to be among the best from the viewpoint of quality: my link with each of them is very strong and aimed at defining a true programming. I feel it is my job to create a collection on the drawing board, with a limited number of fabrics, carefully calculated costs and a flexible styling that will allow the manufacturer the maximum of efficiency (for example in choosing the sources of material for the product). Thus control of the image and the distribution, a guarantee not to do a product to death and an awareness of the dimension of a label with consequent respect of the possible scale of production represent the valid criteria of evaluation which a true fashion designer cannot do without.

9.
GFF, F/W 1996-97

10.
Gianfranco Ferré
Prêt-à-Porter,
F/W 1996-97

11.
Gianfranco Ferré
Prêt-à-Porter,
F/W 1996-97

12.
Gianfranco Ferré
Prêt-à-porter,
F/W 1996-1997

13.
Gianfranco Ferré
Prêt-à-Porter,
F/W 1996-97

14.
GFF,
F/W 1996-97

Materials of the highest quality and sophisticated techniques of manufacture are undoubtedly elements that contribute to the immediate identification of the luxury *prêt-à-porter* garment. But they are also the results of a profoundly different approach to the one taken in the high-fashion atelier, of a culture of clothing that has other roots and other prospects of production. In *prêt-à-porter* the basic condition that guides the quest for elegance is necessarily related to the concrete realization of the garment, put together by machines in standard sizes. Particular structural solutions–the padding of a shoulder, the fitting of a jacket at the waist, the way a pair of pants falls–are made possible if technology provides the means to achieve them. The same is true for the treatment of materials–greater pliability of leather, greater adherence by stretch fabrics, greater lightness of silk–or choices of color. Ascertaining the feasibility of each of these industrial processes also signifies checking costs, lead times and environmental impact. I can say without a shadow

of doubt that the relationship with the industrial dimension is anything but limiting. The contact and constant rapport with the partner-manufacturer represent a powerful stimulus to the search for solutions that will continually improve the quality of the product. A relationship that has in fact enriched both sides. The system of production–I am referring to the Italian one in particular, which I am obviously more familiar with–has absorbed ideas, a taste for experimentation and a desire for originality. In exchange, it has made available an agile structure capable of taking this kind of input on board. A structure in which a balanced integration has been attained between the technological component and the human factor, heir to a tradition of craftsmanship that has fortunately never been forgotten. Ready-to-wear has to give industry the credit for adding quality to the handling of the detail, to the use of the material, to the making of the garment. I will conclude with a very simple observation, in the twofold guise of *créateur* and *couturier*. In my daily activity throughout these years I have never believed in a hard and fast separation between the two spheres of creative action, that they are incompatible or in conflict. Certainly both *haute couture* and *prêt-à-porter* have their peculiarities–the atelier its rituals, industrial design its necessities of production–but I can say with complete confidence that I would not have achieved certain results, not have been able to act with stylistic coherence and consistency, if I had not always made an effort to integrate the experiences gained in both sectors, if I had not been able to transfer with flexibility methods, procedures and stratagems from one field to the other. Starting out from ready-to-wear, it has been almost natural for me to apply a design method in high fashion too, conceiving the collections as a set of garments that are unique but linked by a guiding thread, by a common logic of style. In the opposite direction, I have tried to apply the "riches" of high fashion, the passionate care for detail and for decoration, in ready-to-wear too, adapting them of course to the rules of industrial production. An attitude that comes to me naturally and that will therefore continue to characterize my work, even now, at the end of the exceptional experience with Dior over the last eight years. I have spoken of flexibility, something which now, on the threshold of the 21st century, also means knowing how to broaden the view, knowing how to grasp the desire for change and the continual evolution that shape our lives. Becoming aware of this reality has meant deciding to dedicate my attention and my experience to a new line, Gieffeffe, intended for a wider market, for those who want to feel young, free and uninhibited, finding quality at accessible prices (in the same way, the new Gieffeffe fragrance and the Gianfranco Ferré Jeans line represent responses "in parallel"– that is to say responses which can coexist within an overall project of style carried out on different levels–to needs and desires that are more fluid than ever). I have never betrayed my "origins" as an architect. I have never ceased to be, in all these years, a designer of objects too. I have had extraordinary experiences in high fashion. I know that the journey I have made will help me to understand the future and to interpret it with imagination. And how can I now make a contribution to identifying the most useful means, the most fruitful ways of understanding and interpreting the future? By analyzing the methods and procedures, the aspects of design and the characteristics of a journey that has essentially been one of work in the best and noblest sense, I hope to have got across the idea of just how important it is to "communicate fashion" as a sum of experiences and abilities, as passion for and attention to reality, as capacity for application and inventiveness, as love of the past and tradition and the desire to find out more about them, but without feeling compelled to uncritically reproduce styles and forms that are not longer relevant to our time. The most useful instrument for interpreting the future is the awareness of an original vision of clothing as an aspect of the way we live. It is the personal and rigorous formulation of a method that is founded on the search for formal solutions which will enhance comfort and naturalness, on experimentation with unprecedented choices when it comes to material. It is the desire for new horizons.

Milan, March 14, 1997
Composition and Fashion
Milan Polytechnic. Seminar of the courses in Theories and Techniques of Architecture entitled *Composition in the Practice of Art*

1.
Gianfranco Ferré
Prêt-à-porter,
S/S 1992

I often find myself talking to young people about my work. On my trips overseas I always try to include lectures and meetings with students at fashion or design schools in the schedule. Before taking on the post of artistic director of Maison Dior, I taught courses in Clothing Design at the Domus Academy in Milan for five years, with great pleasure and, I believe, positive results.

It is with emotion that I find myself talking today to students at what used to be my own school many years ago, a place I had entered with fairly confused ideas, but with a great passion for design. A passion that I had to cultivate through constant practice, exercise and application, admiring those of my companions who seemed to me extraordinarily and unattainably better than I was. I emerged from this school with somewhat clearer ideas: paradoxically I had come to the conclusion that I was never going to work in architecture, nor in interior design. I had already created my very first objects: jewelry and accessories in a style that was unusual at the time and that I gave to my female friends and fellow students. I knew nothing about fashion, but I was fascinated by the idea of being able to embellish a body with something I had created, molding the material and playing with it. I was never to work as an architect, but I can say with confidence that, over these twenty-five years, each of my creations has had in it at least a bit–and often much more–of what I learned at Milan Polytechnic. In terms of logic, method and approach to design, but also in terms of willingness to analyze, taste for experimentation and rigor of intentions.

Of course, someone is going to object, fashion is not just this, but is fantasy, intuition, imagination in the pure state too. For me too fashion has two souls. It is both emotion and reason: this is what I would like to talk about here, taking it one precise point at a time and remaining faithful to the principles of analysis that I learned in this very place.

COMPOSITION IN FASHION. THE RULES

Clothing as design, construction and intervention in forms
I have one prime conviction, acquired right here in this school. A fundamental legacy that I never tire of affirming and asserting, in the concrete and daily practice of my work as well as in the ideas and theoretical principles that inform and give meaning to what I do. Creating fashion is certainly an operation of the imagination, an expression of sensitivity and intuition, but indispensable to it is the contribution of method, an aptitude for design that is founded on the conception of the garment as the result of a planned and conscious intervention in forms. An elaboration of simple, elementary forms that leads to intentionally complex and intricate results (figs 2, 3, 4, 5). A process of construction that starts out from a two-dimensional reality–that of the design traced on paper in the form of a drawing–but with the human body as an indispensable referent from the very beginning. The human body as a three-dimensional entity *par excellence*, with its physicality, its real requirements of movement, its dynamics of relationship with what covers it and with the surrounding environment. I am an architect, but I do not build houses or work on their decoration. Nevertheless, for over twenty years, my work has led me to deal every day with forms, those of our body and those of the materials that I use to "construct" the object-garment and that I combine and make compatible

with one another. I strive to condense dreams and emotions, impressions and passions into my clothing, and at the same time I inevitably think in terms of fall and volume, of structures and geometries that give the clothing an identity, a substance and a logic.

Creating clothing means composing forms and taking them apart, analyzing and understanding them, utilizing them and selecting them to arrive at the desired effect. Like an architect, I have to think and act by setting my ideas in the dimension of space.

Clothing as an expression of culture. Fashion as awareness of reality, of the present, of the past

Composing means coming up with an original expression of your own, one which associates a content with a form. A completely new expression with respect to what has previously been "composed" by others. But its content necessarily feeds on external inputs: stimuli, inspirations, references to what goes on in reality, allusions to experiences of earlier times or different origins.

Through my clothes, my collections, the style that I have developed over the years, moves my understanding of life. The work of research that leads me to conceive the garments in their individuality and the collections in their overall expression takes the form of an elaboration of inspirations and ideas of different origin and nature. These last derive in the first place from a precise sense of the reality of our time: fashion design does not signify withdrawing into yourself, shutting yourself up in an ivory tower, basking in a sterile and elitist sense of beauty. Fashion lives in reality. It is an expression of it, drawing its contents from it.

In my clothing I have tried always to give concrete form to the elements and the patterns of behavior that are most characteristic of the way we live: the need for comfort in the first place, the sense of freedom, the necessity of dynamism and speed, pleasure experienced with a greater immediacy and awareness than in the past, naturalness as a well-established attitude. In my intentions, the clothes are interpretations,

2.
Gianfranco Ferré
Prêt-à-Porter,
S/S 1997
black India ink
felt-tip pen on
cardboard

3.
Gianfranco Ferré
Prêt-à-Porter, S/S 1997

4.
Gianfranco Ferré
Prêt-à-Porter, S/S 1997

5.
Gianfranco Ferré
Prêt-à-Porter, F/W 1994-95

6.
Gianfranco Ferré
Prêt-à-Porter,
F/W 1994-95

7.
Dior Couture,
A/W 1996-1997

8.
Gianfranco Ferré
Prêt-à-porter,
A/W 1993-1994

9.
Dior Couture,
A/W 1994-1995

responses to desires and needs, embodiments of moods and aspirations. But fashion also feeds on different experiences. On experiences gained in other fields of human knowledge (especially art), in other moments of our history, in other parts of the world, under other cultural conditions. Without indulging in the slightest in the pleasure of nostalgia–personally I don't find it a pleasure at all, and neither do I think that it can help in any way to give a modern sense to creativity–my style incorporates a broad range of influences. Influences that come from the figurative arts, ranging from great classical painting to the powerful and spare sensibility of the moderns (fig. 6); that come from the worlds and cultures I have got to know and love, in the first place the Orient of India (fig. 7), China and Japan; that come from the great cultural experiences of our past–the baroque, neoclassicism and romanticism (fig. 8); and from the great lessons of elegance that have left their mark on all of us and that include names like Dior, Balenciaga or Worth, along with the common heritage of couture and refinement characteristic of the European style (fig. 9). In my view, fashion cannot be a sterile cult of the past. Rather it is an extraordinary expression of love for the past and for tradition. An avowed love of what tradition is able to transmit and communicate to the sensibility of today.

Clothing and design as self-expression. Your own vocabulary and ideas as the basis of creativity
I think it is fundamental to take stimuli on board, to feed on influences and impressions, to gain from varied and mixed experiences in order to develop an expressive code of your own. A vocabulary of your own, an alphabet, an organized stylistic code that can manifest itself in endless variants, can evolve in time, become enriched, absorb new stimuli, while remaining consistent and true to itself. This is a practical attitude and a methodological approach which can be used to sum up my creative experience over all these years.
It is not difficult to identify signs of this coherence in the now numerous

collections that have followed one another over the seasons. This is the Ferré language: the constant input of tailoring skills into the collections of women's wear as well as those of menswear, the passion for pure and clean colors, the love of precious and noble materials enriched by continual experimentation and innovation, the intelligent interplay between masculine and feminine. It is the pleasure of rediscovering elements in each collection that are timeless and give a precise sense of continuity, of consistency, of fidelity to an idea of beauty: white blouses, narrow pants, see-through effects, "masculine" jackets and suits, leather that is at once forceful and soft, clothing that makes the most of the body, the delight of red, of gold (figs. 10, 11).

COMPOSITION IN FASHION. THE MEANS

The drawing as first step in the design
The drawing is the first concrete expression of an idea. A first point of arrival in the dimension of reality and a point of departure for a design. It is a necessity, as well as a passion. It serves to fix impressions and give them a hint of substance. In a rapid sketch a few precise and succinct lines take form, a silhouette is captured in its essential points–the shoulders, the waist, the legs– which are laid out on the sheet of paper. A few lines that in the phase which comes immediately afterward are developed according to the principles of geometry into a technical drawing, in which the forms and the details of the clothing are reduced and analyzed in elementary terms, in which the measurements and proportions take on definite outlines, so that the whole thing can be read and understood.

The material. Treatments and processing. Technology and research
I never tire of repeating it: the real frontier of fashion of today lies in the relationship between the creative intention and research into materials.

10.
Gianfranco Ferré
Prêt-à-porter,
A/W 1988-1989

11.
Gianfranco Ferré
Prêt-à-porter,
A/W 1986-1987

12.
Gianfranco Ferré
Prêt-à-porter,
A/W 1995-1996

13.
Gianfranco Ferré
Prêt-à-porter,
S/S 1995

14.
Gianfranco Ferré
Prêt-à-porter,
A/W 1991-1992

15.
Gianfranco Ferré
Prêt-à-porter,
A/W 1992-1993

16.
Gianfranco Ferré
Prêt-à-porter,
A/W 1995-1996

17.
Gianfranco Ferré
Prêt-à-porter,
S/S 1992

The success, the fruitful handling of this relationship, gives fashion contents of the present and guarantees for the future.

Fashion derives its substance and even its physical and tangible existence from the material. I can say with confidence that a fundamental part of my creative effort has always taken the form of an innovative and constantly "curious" approach to material. Technological experimentation offers unheard-of possibilities for the utilization of materials, "invents" new ones, optimizes their qualities and potentialities, and makes possible unprecedented mixes, combinations and treatments: ones that were actually inconceivable until a few decades ago.

The importance of the input from technology goes beyond its pragmatic sphere of application. It is the manifestation of a new character, of a new identity of fashion. Today's fashion necessarily looks to the future, thinks in terms of progress and feeds on advances in technology, after having explored, revived and assimilated all the experiences of style and taste already consolidated in the past. The advances in technology give a concrete connotation to the new opportunities for creativity, the ingredients of which the designer makes use in order to "compose": procedures and processes that make possible more flexible structural solutions (less rigid padding of the shoulders, truly figure-hugging clothes, natural and at the same time impeccable falls) and cutting-edge interventions on the material (a greater adherence on the part of stretch fabrics, fig. 12, a greater pliability of leather, fig. 13, a greater lightness of silk, double texture proofing that makes the garment warmer without increasing its weight at all).

Our fashion (I am referring to Italian ready-to-wear in particular, with its solid industrial background and its entrepreneurial roots) benefits more from this "technological prospect" than that of other countries, as it can count on the extraordinary skills offered by our manufacturing system. Focused by tradition and constitution on the activity of processing, our industry, and the textile industry in particular, is able here to make the most of its familiarity with experimentation, its quickness in adopting and making its own the innovative inputs that come from the creative side.

Color, an "intrinsic" element of design
Along with the material, color is the basic element on which the designer draws to compose. Color represents an inseparable category with respect to the idea of the garment, to its form and its nature, right from the very first idea and the very first sketch on paper.

My colors are already part of the inspiration at the moment in which it starts to take shape. I have already mentioned the Ferré vocabulary, which is the coherent set of "signs" that can easily be identified in the collections and that characterize my style. Colors are a natural and fundamental part of this lexicon.

Intentional and necessary, Ferré colors display a character that remains faithful over time, even though capable of infinite modulations season after season. On clear and well-defined bases it is possible to discern each year new shades and highlights, surprising tones and nuances that form in turn a more multifaceted vocabulary of their own that expresses energy, poetry, magic, allure, purity. A chromatic lexicon that, in the practical procedure of the work, is constructed with experimental methods, by means of successive trials that aim to bring the desire–the desired shade–closer to reality. A method that is naturally also applied to the material aspect, through an often complex series of phases, of minimal but constant advances toward the intended result.

So it is on clear and well-defined bases that the absolute colors and non-colors move. The colors I have always used–white, black, red, blue, natural shades, gold–and, from time to time, the glow of metals, the intense glints of semiprecious stones, flashes of energetic hues, the delicacy of the tints of dawn and of flowers. For composing also means always being able to surprise (figs. 14, 15, 16, 17).

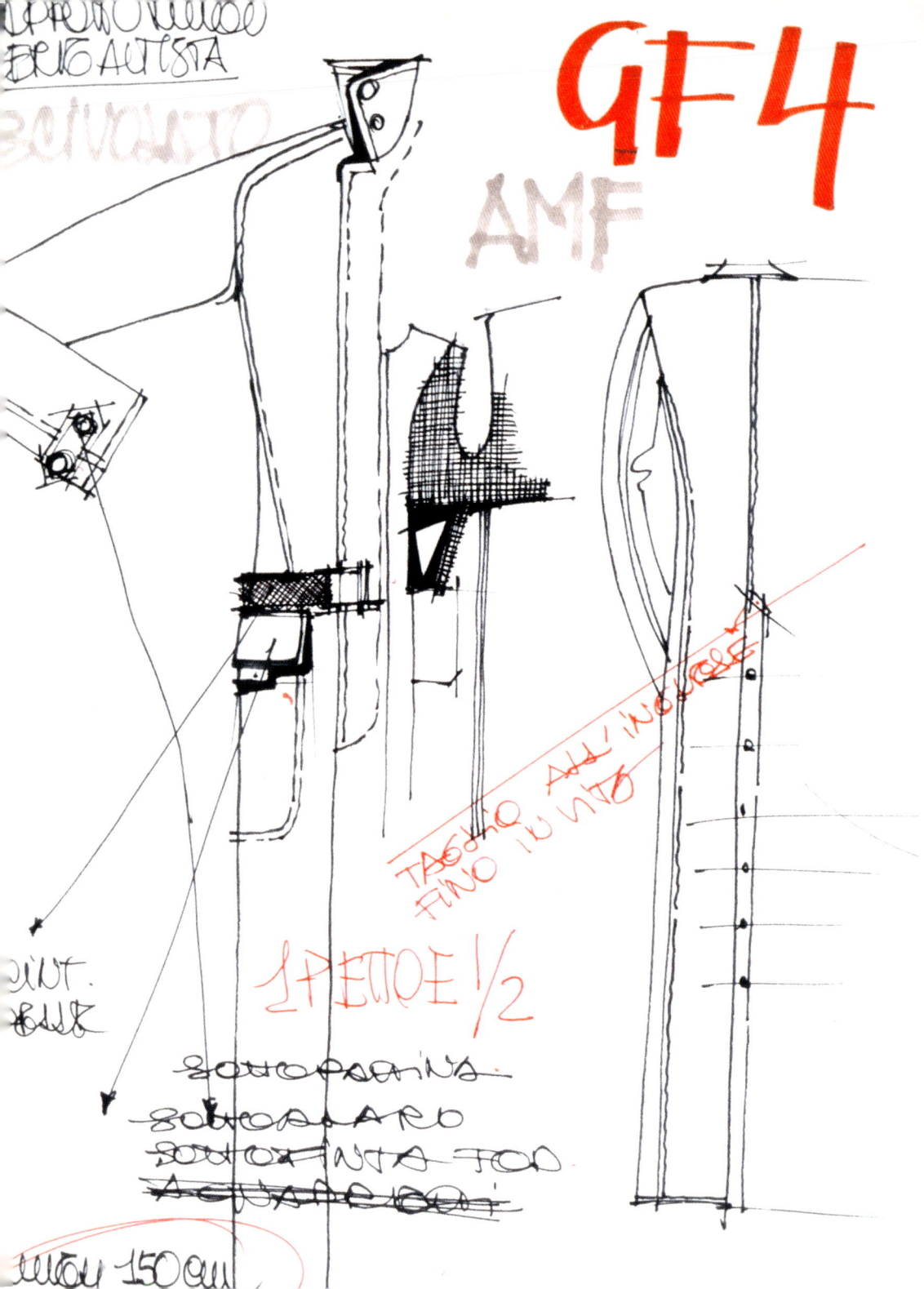

THE COMPOSITION OF FASHION. THE ENDS

The garment as product and as utilitarian object. The sense of reality
Not unlike a book or a movie and perhaps with a "reason for its use" that is even more deeply rooted in everyday life, the garment has a very precise function as a "utilitarian object." It is possible to expatiate at length on primary needs and choices of a superfluous nature, on the fact that today anyone who buys an item of clothing, especially at the level of those offered by our *prêt-à-porter* or even by *haute couture*, does so more for pleasure than out of necessity. There are many today who put forward the "full closets" argument: we all possess large quantities of clothes and so they are no longer necessities.

To a degree, I believe that there are elements of truth in all this. Over the last decade clothing has lost much of its value as a status symbol, and consumption, already reduced by the recession, is now channeled toward other "objects of desire": travel, vacations, culture, technology.

These are undeniable facts, and ones which affect all advanced societies in more or less the same way. Likewise, I am inclined to believe that, if clothing has ceased to be "the object of desire" *par excellence*, a vehicle for the display of a prosperity acquired or a social status attained, then it is all the more necessary to think of it and conceive it as an object of real use. In other words as a product that in a changing system of values and interests continues to be desirable because it offers certain guarantees: qualities, duration, a good price/quality relationship, elements of uniqueness that render it interesting, and therefore necessary, even given the large quantity of clothes that are already hanging in our wardrobes. Thus "composing fashion" signifies treating the garment as a product (one that is mass produced in ready-to-wear, but has an exclusive character in high fashion), as a concrete outlet for the desire to invest in something that embodies precise values and contents. Creating an item of clothing signifies conceiving it right from the outset as something that will be worn, that will be able to meet real and everyday requirements,

18.
Gianfranco Ferré
prêt-à-porter
A/W 1997-1998
black felt-tip pen
India ink on paper

that will be chosen and identified as a suitable response to a need, in the same way as a book or a movie are conceived and made to be read and seen respectively. I can say this on the basis of a more than consolidated experience, and this attitude is as typical of my approach to factory-made *prêt-à-porter* as it is of that to *haute couture*. In both dimensions my clothes are the fruit of a balance that I strive to achieve between an expression of individuality (my "interpretation" of life) and the objective conditions that allow my creative intention to become a product: in ready-to-wear the rules and requirements of industrial mass production of the garment, in high fashion its real specificities, that is to say the concrete needs that have brought the customer to the atelier.

Clothing as a quest for effect, as a vehicle of feelings and means of expression
Notwithstanding what I have just said about the real and concrete essence of the garment understood as a utilitarian object, as well as an element and source of creative enrichment, I consider the pursuit of an eye-catching effect to be of great importance, as origin and first moment of inspiration for the clothing itself. A quest that leads you, for instance, to imagine the garment as a splotch of color, as a glow of light that shifts with the movement of the body, as an illusory and alchemical play of materials, as an elusive, intangible silhouette, defined only by its symbiotic overlap with the figure and with its natural forms, as emphasis of a detail intended bestow the magic of exclusivity on the absolute linearity of the garment as a whole. It is the search for an effect as creative stimulus, as elucidation of a play of illusion that nonetheless never loses sight of an awareness of reality (figs.19, 20, 21).

COMPOSITION IN FASHION. THE PRESENT, THE FUTURE

In my attempt to explain how the process of composition can be applied to the realm of fashion, I have so far proceeded by analysis, naturally making reference to my personal and professional experience. However, I would like to stress that the contents I have pointed out possess a sort of general validity that directly concerns all my work. They are aspects of my creativity that, to some extent, have a timeless character and that, precisely for this reason, constitute the fundamental framework of my approach to the composition of clothing. A timeless character that naturally makes them indispensable within the whole range of aesthetic references and that is a guarantee of fidelity over time to myself and to my personal development of a style.

To bring this discourse to a conclusion, I would like to analyze more closely the signs of evolution that breathe life into the present and that I believe will also inspire the imminent future, in the sphere of taste and dress: evolution of taste in general, and of my taste and my relationship with the idea of fashion in particular. Proceeding once again point by point, I will present my thoughts in fairly concise form, more as ideas on which we can reflect together than as the "manual" of a style.

I would like, at this point, to make two preliminary observations before going into detail. Skeptical with regard to any ambition of drastic rupture and radical change, I am a keen supporter of the principle of constant and progressive modification of taste and custom, made up–from day to day and season to season–of small steps forward, of tiny, sometimes barely perceptible alterations, on which the future of fashion is built. The elements that characterize my style in the present, are not "born today." They are not in conflict with what I do not hesitate to define as my "same old" style. They do not in any way represent a desire to break with the course of my creative development and the convictions that lie behind it. In the second place, whereas up to now I have referred exclusively to the collections of women's and men's *prêt-à-porter* and the *haute couture* that I designed for Christian Dior for eight years, the reflections that follow will unavoidably be extended to the new lines that I have launched recently, Gieffeffe and Gianfranco Ferré Jeans in particular. A necessary attitude of elasticity has led me to channel my experience into these new areas, with the intention of offering and guaranteeing quality contents to a broader segment of the market, to a public that is looking chiefly for freedom and casualness in clothing.

19.
Dior Couture,
S/S 1996

20.
Gianfranco Ferré
Prêt-à-porter,
S/S 1997

21.
Gianfranco Ferré
Prêt-à-porter,
S/S 1997

THE NEW VALUES: FREEDOM, COMFORT, NATURALNESS

The first value: the body
Freedom, comfort and naturalness are certainly not new factors in my approach to design. The body has always been an absolute value. My clothes are created to dress living, moving figures that have precise requirements of freedom and comfort. Over the years I have accentuated the attention I pay to these values, aiming at an even more marked simplification of the lines, deliberately eliminating any trace of superfluity and creating slender and essential, fluid and flowing silhouettes (fig. 22),

22.
Gianfranco Ferré
Prêt-à-porter,
S/S 1997

23.
Gianfranco Ferré
Prêt-à-porter,
S/S 1997

hugging the figure as a result of the adherence provided by the cuts and to an even greater extent by the material, whose elastic fibers offer a new look and a remarkable pliability. My vocabulary for the future is oriented toward the value of simplicity and the rejection of clothing as "encumbrance."

The quest for simplicity also takes the form of a deliberate elimination of the bulk of the garment which is oversized with respect al body.
I design smaller shoulders, softened by the desire for naturalness. The waist is marked, but not emphasized. The pants docilely follow the line of the legs. The skirts have fluctuating lengths, decidedly short or decidedly long, but in any case interchangeable on the basis of taste, of pleasure, of an absolute sense of freedom. My clothes, and certain blouses in particular, may retain deliberate traces of opulence, large and emphatic volumes, but are always endowed with a lightness that liberates you from any sense of encumbrance and constriction.

The garment as individual "piece" within the collection
As part of a constant and consistent process of evolution, the principle of a growing independence of the individual garments with respect to one another, as well as in their relationship to the spirit of the collection as a whole, has emerged within my collections over time.
I am inclined to conceive the collection itself as a set of individual elements that can be used and combined without being subject to preestablished conditionings. A range of clothes with a fluid tendency, characterized by precise and coherent elements of identification. The leitmotiv of a unique style subtly pervades my collections, but my clothes are born today as "free pieces." And freedom governs the relationship between the basic typologies of clothing: the blouse can turn into a jacket, the jacket lengthen to become a duster coat, the pants of the suit be cut down into shorts, the jeans be given a more precious character or turned into an object of technological experimentation.

The principle of superimposition and stratification
The relationship with the body is changing, the requirements that clothing has to meet are changing, and so the need for people to cover themselves is changing even in relation to the different character of the seasons and to alterations in the climate. I believe that today dressing continues to mean covering the body, but also–depending on the needs and the moment–uncovering it, superimposing "pieces," alternating them, putting them together and assembling them in layers, on the basis of freer and easier combinations, motivated by a desire for wellbeing and comfort. Superimposition becomes play, means of seduction, poetic allusion and evocation of new delicacies, of an unprecedented romanticism that speaks of clarity and freshness (fig. 23).

The breakdown of the barriers between daywear and eveningwear
The free and conscious use of clothing is demolishing the principle of a rigid and binding separation between the day and the evening.

24.
Gianfranco Ferré
Prêt-à-porter,
S/S 1997

In response to this development, I am proposing precious materials, marked lengths and echoes of poetry for use in the daytime as well. In the evening, bare legs, absolute simplicity, exaltation of the body.

Decoration as personal choice
Composing with the goals of simplification, essentiality and cleanness of line signifies leaving to individual taste the pleasure of decoration, the touch of originality, the freedom to interpret a style. From my aesthetic perspective decoration has the fundamental value of an eccentric choice, a real affirmation of the self in dressing, which cannot be passively made to conform to "prepackaged" canons and models. A prominent piece of jewelry, a belt or an accessory is an expression of feeling and intelligence, with respect to which the designer can do no more than make attractive suggestions which each person can accept or decline.

Style on different and complementary levels: the first line, the "second lines," the youth lines, the sports lines
These are definitions of a necessarily generic character that are perhaps not much help in grasping the true nature of the lines that are produced alongside the ready-to-wear one and that arise out of partnerships with leading companies in the clothing sector: Marzotto for Gieffeffe and Gianfranco Ferré Studio, ITJ-Ittierre for Gianfranco Ferré Jeans.
In the face of the fluidity of needs and the shifting dynamics of taste, the division of the style into different levels represents a real acid test for the designer and his ability to "compose" in a constructive relationship with reality. Different levels that in fact I have always taken into consideration in my work. My very first line of casual clothing, Oaks, was actually brought out simultaneously with my women's ready-to-wear line in 1978; my link with Marzotto has already gone past the momentous turning point of its tenth anniversary and even jeans are not a completely new experience for me.
Yet I think that in the present situation the designer should assign

greater weight to these dimensions. And for an extremely simple series of reasons that it is possible, I believe, to sum up in the following observation: since these collections are born out of cooperation with large-scale industry, the resort to technological experimentation appears easier and more natural. It is possible to think in terms of large numbers and an ever more marked rationalization of production. So you can also aim at broader targets, at larger segments of the market, with prices and costs of a radically different nature from the ones usually associated with luxury *prêt-à-porter*.

It is possible to imagine a truly all-inclusive project of style, modulated on different levels, all interconnected with each other, in which parallel responses–the various lines and collections–take shape that are characterized by evident common aesthetic references, but in actual fact are differentiated by heterogeneous materials and procedures, and therefore have different costs, prices and channels of distribution.

This is the terrain on which style is tracing its indications for the future. A challenging terrain that sees me playing a leading role with a particularly intense involvement right now, at the conclusion of my "adventure" with Dior. With great commitment and with a great sense of satisfaction over the whole range of stimuli and inputs that this new set of references is bringing to my creative experience, to my capacity to compose.

Tokio, June 12, 1997
Men's Fashion
United Nations University

1.
Gianfranco Ferré
Prêt-à-porter,
A/W 1992-1993

Men's fashion is for me, above all, a question of method. The approach is rooted in design: in this sense my training as an architect has provided me with the mental aptitude and with means, including cultural resources and research tools, that are perfectly suited to the microcosm of fashion. The basic idea behind my analysis of men's fashion lies in the constant search for proposals that are flexible, but always offer the utmost comfort, that hark back to a distant, but still present, origin in traditional manners, just as my approach to menswear is traditional: I have always studied and created it with a naturalness that, perfecting the concept of the supple and unstructured garment, has now become my "familiar lexicon." And these seem to me to be precise and recognizable connotations of masculine elegance.
I like to experiment with technological combinations of materials or to try grafting forms inspired by the world of sport, almost as if it were a challenge that I have set myself. Sometimes the leading role is played by color, vivid, strong and clear, but very masculine, typical of Napoleonic military standards and uniforms; or by marked and expressive stripes on shirts and on club neckties, reinvented and bold, in a vaguely campus spirit. It is a quest for nobility, a lively classicism, not puffed-up or boring but a true expression of freedom, while remaining conscious of tradition (figs. 1, 2, 3, 4, 5).
I would like the Gianfranco Ferré line of menswear to express these precise, personal connotations, but with a touch of severity. Every color

fits with my own, tried-and-tested scheme of traditions: blue where the use of blue is prescribed, gray or charcoal when custom would have it, but also total white or desert sand with the vaguely colonial feeling of a short story by Paul Bowles.

While I love the experimentation and research carried out in the field of sports (fig. 7), vacation or leisure wear (fig. 6), I believe in the symbolic and representative value contained in formal clothing, in the classical which has a precise identity, since dressing for town has codified, conformist rules. Just like leisure wear, it is subject to excursions in a metaphorical sense too, where a hint of irony and amusement is allowed. And then it is not impossible for certain experiences and forms of typological research to be transferred from one theme to another, in an attempt to come up with new solutions. Yet I am convinced that what most inflates the fashion world is the always new, the new at any cost, something which–moreover–immediately looks old and outdated.

2.
Gianfranco Ferré
Prêt-à-porter,
A/W 1995-1996

3.
Gianfranco Ferré
Prêt-à-porter,
S/S 1983

4.
Gianfranco Ferré
Prêt-à-porter,
S/S 1996

5.
Gianfranco Ferré
Prêt-à-porter,
S/S 1987

6.
Gianfranco Ferré
Prêt-à-porter,
S/S 1993

When designing clothes I always take the route of the sensations, a secret thread that links one emotion to the next and to the logic of taste rather than reason. The classic values of men's clothing are inescapable points of a cultural training not forced into schemes and categories: so yes to the casual, as it signifies comfort and brings back the long stride of the twenty-year-old; yes to conservatism because creates an image and hints at success; yes to a creative touch because it denotes the unconventional and bold spirit of a man in touch with his own time.

Looking back over the history of men's clothing, it is clear that everything has already been thought of and tried out: from the vain 18th century when every extreme of frivolity was admissible (vests of brocade, lace and embroidery) to a severe Catholic and Victorian 19th century characterized by the exclusive use of black, but also a time when men wore ritual clothing, emblematic interpreters of every occasion and event; from the taste for luxury and the unconventional of the early 20th

Gianfranco Ferré

7.
Gianfranco Ferré
Prêt-à-porter,
S/S 1994

8.
Gianfranco Ferré
Prêt-à-porter,
A/W 1995-1996

9.
Gianfranco Ferré
Prêt-à-porter,
S/S 1997

10.
Gianfranco Ferré
Prêt-à-porter,
S/S 1986

11.
Gianfranco Ferré
Prêt-à-porter,
A/W 1984-1985

12.
Gianfranco Ferré
Prêt-à-porter,
A/W 1994-1995

13.
Gianfranco Ferré
Prêt-à-porter,
A/W 1995-1996

century with its wild, literary, bohemian spirit to the extraordinary (figs. 8, 9, 10), innovative Neapolitan tailoring tradition of the thirties.
And it is to the cult of sartorial elegance that I have harked back ideally, redefining themes and rules laid down over time and reinterpreting them in a modern key, typical of the tradition of Gianfranco Ferré clothes. And then I have gone further, perfecting the concept of suppleness, of the unstructured garment, perhaps deliberately adding a touch of eccentricity. And I did this not out of pure snobbery, but as a complete mental reorganization of the themes that have always existed in menswear. In my primer reemerge and return concepts like tradition, calm, confidence, luxury (in the cashmere loden coat, in the blue blazer with precious buttons) and respect for cuts and colors, but set in an absolutely contemporary and modern climate (figs. 11, 12, 13).
I retrace some personal sources of inspiration and like to think of myself as eccentric, but also austere, solidly Lombard in my attitudes and sentiments, while profoundly Central European in my reading and culture. Ironically I could throw into the mix a few good movies by Ivory and Merchant, novels by Forster, books by Kipling, extracts of letters from Virginia Woolf to Vita Sackville-West. A total proposition that privileges tradition and quality, that rejects the frantic search for the fashionable idea in order to tackle with rigor the broader and more general, in a certain absolute sense, quest for that of dressing with style.
So each Gianfranco Ferré collection can be said to be recognizable: canonical themes are revived and reworked; natural, typically masculine colors emerge; a mode, an attitude is declined, as if the clothes were words that make up a familiar and recognizable language, a constant vocabulary. To sum up, I could say movement, action, attention to detail, research into material and an ancient artisan uniqueness translated into modern accents, in the construction of a male wardrobe that generates different styles, mutable approaches to elegance and independence of choice, but always traced back to our clear European roots, for this civilization of ours has been decisive in shaping the forms of men's

clothing. The reality of our time is a physical reality, a reality of adaptation of products that cut across the times, without being targeted at a single season.

I like to think I am working on an all-inclusive project that puts objects "into orbit" around the world of men; not just clothes, therefore, but accessories that require study and intuition of the form and the *modus*, mode or modality, in which to design and use the objects themselves. These are sunglasses and neckties that I like to design and collect: neckties synonymous with tradition and extremism, but also with fantasy and style, whether they sport stripes, polka dots or paisley patterns. And again a range of leather goods that imply good habits and elegantly masculine gestures, from the billfold to suitcases hand-stitched in Piacenza, the historic center of the saddleries of the ducal army: a great craft and family culture, handed down from father to son. Culminating in the fragrances, not just for an unattainable and sophisticated woman but also for an exacting man who is able to appreciate the design of a bottle, in which care is taken over the smallest details. And again, for the desk of a man whom I like to imagine devoting part of his time to works of the mind, fountain and other pens in silver and lacquer that offer the pleasure, including the tactile one, of the beautiful object.

I think that the future will be an expression of our spirit more than of our power and our money, even if today a "uniform" does not represent so much the status of a person as his mental paradigm.

I like to define my history of "making things for men" as evolution in continuity. Continuity above all in the method of working, in the constant reinterpretation of tradition, in the development of the style, as each collection is shaped by the moment in history, by the social environment in which it is set, by needs, by habits, in short by the way the clothing is used.

Milan, July 14, 1997
Jewelry between East and West, a Balancing of Design and Fantasy
Domus Academy. Fashion Design Summer Session *Fashion and Jewelry*

1.
Gianfranco Ferré
advertising
A/W 1994-1995,
photo Tyen

Jewelry: My First Love

So I made my first jewelry: bracelets, necklaces, brooches, sculptured belts halfway between the accessory and the jewel. Unusual objects for the time, in the vanguard compared to what you could see at the time in the fashion magazines. In a way, they were examples of authentic craftsmanship. The rigor of the forms and the precise sense of design went hand in hand with direct intervention in the material. Leather, metal, plastic: materials that I molded, assembled and modeled by hand. I showed these "objects" to some female friends and fellow students at university, gave them some of them and in the end people in the industry noticed them. They were liked, they made an impression and they were photographed (figs. 2, 3, 4, 5).

(Gianfranco Ferré, *Lettres à un jeune couturier*. Paris: Editions Ballard, 1995)

My adventure in the fashion world began by chance–almost thirty years ago, even before I had finished my architectural studies–more for the pleasure of handling the materials and succeeding in "producing" something original and in keeping with my own taste than out of any conviction that I was suited to the role of a fashion designer. And perhaps it is no coincidence that this adventure started with jewelry. Even at that time the fascination that makes this specific sphere of application of design so interesting and engrossing took concrete form in my eyes in a series of expressive opportunities that were highly distinctive and very close to my understanding of a creative process. It seemed fundamental to me that my intervention entailed direct contact with the material: a relationship based on artisan, "demiurgic" manual skill channeled into the realization of beautiful and original forms, through the modeling of the materials. I already felt, moreover, a strong and decisive impulse to make use of unusual materials, different from the ones traditionally employed in the making of jewelry. It was the sense of challenge, the pleasure of research, the desire to experiment and innovate, to get away from the familiar and probe new possibilities. Something that I feel to be a profound part of my nature and that characterizes my approach to material, the sort that I use to create jewelry no less than the fabrics to which I turn for my clothing. Finally, my creative intervention already manifested itself as a desire to challenge the boundaries between the various types of product: the belt-sculpture, for example, performed the dual function of completing the garment and decorating it; it was at once accessory and jewel, complement and ornament. The redefinition of roles and categories within the horizons

of dress later found much wider application in the field of clothing proper, when I set out to reconsider the differences between shirt and jacket, between swimsuit and precious body for the evening, or between menswear and women's wear and between daywear and eveningwear. So it's not really a coincidence that my adventure started with jewelry. This is borne out by the fact that–almost thirty years later–my passion for jewelry, as a fundamental complement of the garment and means of decoration of the body, has never faded. A passion that has matured and grown, that has been able to multiply and strengthen, binding many other fields of application to itself in a coherent relationship. A passion that, when all is said and done, is still expressed through modes and intentions outlined at the time and that I would now like to describe to you point by point, trying to explain just what it is that, in my opinion, makes the creation of jewelry an extremely stimulating sphere of activity.

Jewelry and Fashion: a Coherent Project
Over time the horizons have expanded: today Ferré jewelry is part of a whole range of elements that gravitate around the clothing, serving to enrich and complement it: bags, belts, shoes, scarves. Expressions of an all-inclusive project of style that is articulated season after season in a relationship which firmly and coherently links each of these "complementary" elements to the clothing-object.
Necessary and inseparable: that is the nature of the relationship between garment and accessory and therefore between garment and jewelry in my collections. Since jewelry and clothing stem from a common inspiration, they are in tune with each other from the very first moment in which a collection starts to take shape. Both spring from the same ideas (even though couched in different forms and materials), the same references, the same horizons. Clothing and jewelry: one is the mirror of the other, one helps to understand and explain the other. A necessary and indivisible connection, therefore, but one that has nothing to do with the suffocating, limiting and above all outdated concept

2.
Gianfranco Ferré
Accessories,
1969-1970

3.
Gianfranco Ferré
Accessories,
1969-1970

4.
Gianfranco Ferré
Accessories,
1969-1970

5.
Gianfranco Ferré
Accessories,
1969-1970

of the "obligatory" accessory, imposed like a diktat, which envisages preestablished and unquestionable associations between that jacket and that brooch, that blouse and that bracelet, that dress and that necklace. On the contrary, in my idea of elegance jewelry has a far more fascinating role. Seen as a decorative element, it becomes a means of interpreting the clothing, of coming up with a subjective and individual reading of the garment. If the item of clothing is the object (the "thing that is worn"), jewelry is an expression of its mode, that is to say of "how it is worn." And I hold to the principle that in the reality of today the "how" should be decided independently, on the basis of your own taste, your own convictions, your desire to feel unique, your wish to feel at ease with a style, thanks to the opportunities that decoration offers to nuance it and adapt it to yourself. Finally, from my creative perspective the function of jewelry is not just to be an expression of an all-inclusive concept of elegance and a way of interpreting the clothing, but also to be

a manifestation of a modern and up-to-date idea of luxury. Rigorous and coherent, capable of articulating the values of refinement and opulence in new forms and projecting them into the future, luxury has always been a legitimate part of my firmest beliefs. And nor can we ignore the fact that luxury has a timeless appeal for women and men. Jewelry is one of its most important expressions, a flexible and versatile way of translating ideas and emotions into reality. Of bringing dreams to life (figs. 6, 7, 8).

Jewelry and Material: Invention and Interpretation

No less than at the outset, the process by which I create my jewelry takes the form of a passion for research. A process in which a taste for constant experimentation prevails, made manifest season after season in the utilization and reinterpretation of "poor" materials, those offered by nature and not in themselves sufficiently valuable or precious, or those defined–in the broad sense–as technological, the offspring of industrial culture and so seen for the most part in terms of their properties and their purely functional characteristics. Materials that, for one reason or another, are extraneous to the tradition of jewelry, and therefore foreign to the world of luxury and its production. Materials that for me instead are fundamental precisely because they are able to bestow a new and modern connotation on luxury, one that is more complex and fluid, more nuanced in character and so richer and more stimulating, for the person who designs it no less than for the person who wears it. A new view of luxury that, however, can be perfectly in keeping with its more established expressions. Like the bracelet made of straw and raffia with small wooden elements (fig. 10) or the rigging of a boat that, interwoven with braiding and combined with metal, creates a new opulence (fig. 9). Ebony and wenge with veining and grooving that recalls bark (fig. 11) or again the synthetic amber that perfectly reproduces the luster and warm gleams of the genuine kind (figs. 12, 13). Despite being a fervent champion of experimentation, I am equally enthusiastic about expressing all my love for and devotion to traditional forms of luxury in my jewelry.

6.
Gianfranco Ferré
advertising
A/W 1993-1994,
photo Tyen

7.
Gianfranco Ferré
advertising
S/S 1990,
photo Gian Paolo
Barbieri

8.
Gianfranco Ferré
advertising
A/W 1991-1992,
photo Gian Paolo
Barbieri

9.
Gianfranco Ferré
advertising
S/S 1989
photo Herb Ritts

10.
Gianfranco Ferré
Prêt-à-porter,
S/S 1993

11.
Gianfranco Ferré
Prêt-à-porter,
S/S 1993

12.
Gianfranco Ferré
Prêt-à-porter,
A/W 1993-1994

13.
Gianfranco Ferré
Prêt-à-porter,
A/W 1993-1994

14.
Gianfranco Ferré
Prêt-à-porter,
A/W 1992-1993
photo Gian Paolo
Barbieri

15.
Gianfranco Ferré
advertising
S/S 1991
photo Gian Paolo
Barbieri

16.
Gianfranco Ferré
advertising
S/S 1991
photo Gian Paolo
Barbieri

New interpretations take their cue from timeless impressions: jewels whose lines are refined and opulent at one and the same time, the gleams of gold, silver and other metals, the glints of gems, rhinestone, jet and coral. Echoes of China in the bracelets and earrings made of gilded metal and the belt of gilded leather (fig. 14), lavish Indian bracelets in gilded metal (fig. 16), gems, paste and pearls (fig. 15), absolute brilliance for the necklace and cuff links decorated with rhinestone and crystals (fig. 1).

Jewelry and Form: the Body Enhanced
The body with its structures and proportions constitutes the prime and fundamental reference for every piece of clothing I design. Right from the first intuition, from the first idea sketched rapidly on paper, the body "lives" in the clothing with its volumes, its three-dimensionality, the sense of movement that brings it to life and makes it real.
In just the same way, my jewelry is linked to the "physicality" of human

17.
Gianfranco Ferré
advertising
S/S 1993
photo Tyen

18.
Gianfranco Ferré
Prêt-à-porter,
A/W 1986-1987

19.
Gianfranco Ferré
Prêt-à-porter,
S/S 1992

20.
Gianfranco Ferré
Prêt-à-porter,
A/W 1993-1994

forms by a profound and essential relationship, characterized by an intention of almost geometric rigor that views jewelry as means of drawing attention to the key points of the figure: the base of the head emphasized by earrings; the neck–which connects the head to the torso and the shoulders and is therefore a "cardinal point" of my silhouette–exalted by necklaces and chains; the arms and wrists ringed with lots of bracelets; the waist marked by jeweled belts, beneath which the legs extend, sinuously. I could even say that in my imagination jewelry helps me to "construct" the body, to sculpt it with clarity, to fix its harmonies and proportions with distinct and prominent signs. Signs that decorate and adorn it, but that, in a way, are also an essential part of it. Simple circles of gilded metal on black indicate the waist (fig. 18); neck and wrists are underlined by the accumulation of necklaces and bracelets in wood and gilded metal (fig. 17). Under the belt-trophy extend the svelte and slender legs of the lean pants (fig. 19). The intensity of the relationship that links jewelry to the body is

also revealed when the piece is called on to emphasize its movements and follow them with fidelity, underlining and softening them, interpreting their grace and harmony and exercising a seductive allure: bracelets that tinkle with the swinging of the arms (fig. 20), the necklace that hangs down to caress the figure, the belt that marks out the rhythm of the hips. Bracelets of gilded metal and gems accumulate on the wrist and jingle in unison.

Jewelry between East and West: Influences and Inspirations
The title I have chosen for this lecture is, in reality, a bit limiting. It has in effect the value and function of a necessary synthesis that embraces much broader and move varied horizons.
East and West: these are just the extreme poles or, better still, two of the many coordinates of the panorama of sources from which Ferré jewelry takes its inspiration. This is without doubt a geographic panorama too, conceivable as a summation of East and West. The latter, represented by the taste for clean and severe forms, by the culture of design that links the jewelry to the clothing and the different pieces of jewelry together in a coherent relationship, by allusions to the great aesthetic and figurative experiences of our past, like the baroque whorls of a choker in gilded and embossed metal (fig. 21). The East, on the contrary, manifests itself as preciosity and magic, in the richness and opulence of the forms, in the glints of metals and gems, in the precise conception that assigns to jewelry the value of a symbol as well as an ornament, in the splendor of India or China, in the martial refinement of Japan. Necklaces, bracelets and other pieces of jewelry in a nickel alloy that recalls Indian silver; an "imperial" necklace in gilded metal with pendants made of Galalith, semiprecious stones and Chinese decorative elements (fig. 22); the rigor of the samurai in the red lacquer and metal bracelet-wristband with gilded edges (fig. 23).
East and West added, however, to an infinite number of other dimensions and influences: those of ethnic derivation, for example, which have inspired me to design strong, primitive and barbaric, often even "totemic" pieces of jewelry, or those related to nature–real or

21.
Gianfranco Ferré advertising A/W 1985-1986, photo Herb Ritts

22.
Gianfranco Ferré Prêt-à-porter, A/W 1993-1994

23.
Gianfranco Ferré Prêt-à-porter, S/S 1986

24.
Gianfranco Ferré Prêt-à-porter, S/S 1993

25.
Gianfranco Ferré Prêt-à-porter, S/S 1989

fantastic, authentic or imagined–which allow me to use flowers, seashells and marine animals to decorate my clothes. "Totemic" necklace-sculpture made of gilded metal embossed with patterns that recall the leaves of the Amazon forest (fig. 24); fantastic flowers made of tulle spattered with sequins (fig. 25); the colors of tropical flowers: bracelet sculpture made of painted wood, gilded metal, paste and semiprecious stones (fig. 30); gilded metal starfish embellish the wrist (fig. 26).

Jewelry and Clothing: from Accessory to Complement
The free play of fantasy and the desire to try out new expressions of style characterize a specific interpretation of jewelry that runs through my collections as an authentic leitmotiv, with innovative results that–I think I can say without being accused of a lack of modesty–have left a mark on the fashion of these years, even becoming an integral part of the way elegance is concieved in our time. From my creative perspective, jewelry has always

26.
Gianfranco Ferré
advertising
S/S 1988
photo Herb Ritts

27.
Gianfranco Ferré
Prêt-à-porter,
A/W 1994-1995

28.
Gianfranco Ferré
Prêt-à-porter,
A/W 1992-1993

29.
Gianfranco Ferré
Prêt-à-porter,
S/S 1993

30.
Gianfranco Ferré
advertising
S/S 1993
photo Gian Paolo
Barbieri

coincided with the accessory, and can also be the essential complement, the characteristic and distinguishing detail of a garment. The jewel belt (at once accessory and jewelry) and the jewel button (simultaneously detail of the clothing and jewelry) are elements that it is not hard to identify, despite their variations and their different interpretations, in the chronological succession of my collections, and that, as I have said, have now become part of common taste and not just that of the customers who buy my products. "Cascades" of paste and crystals for the belt-jewel that brightens up the rigor of the gray (fig. 27). The jewel-accessory and the jewel buttons with a thousand decorations: in paste on the precious jacket, in gilded and embossed metal on the black leather jacket and hyper-feminine dress (fig. 28). Deliberately taking this conception to extremes, I have obtained even more singular results. Jewelry, heightened and emphasized in its form and dimension, can replace the clothing, or at least part of it. It can be used to "dress" and cover the body, laid directly on top of the bare flesh (fig. 29).

London, November 26, 1998
Designing the Material
Central Saint Martin's College of Art & Design. Phoenix Theatre

1.
Gianfranco Ferré
Prêt-à-porter,
S/S 1990

I believe that quite independently of the professional sphere in which you work there is a particular value in handing on your own know-how to those who are intending to go down the same route. It is a source of satisfaction to discover that your experience can be of help in identifying the modes and forms of a certain working environment, especially if it is one that involves creativity.

Passing on knowledge also signifies getting across the idea of a method, a system and a manner of proceeding, all of which are indispensable for the development of any project. But, even more important, transmitting knowledge is an investment. A guarantee of continuity for your own work: the assurance that your own "achievements" can be built on, developed and spread, so that they become part of a common heritage of creativity and culture. And creativity and culture are highly dependent on continuity.

From a perspective that embraces and amalgamates present and future, I think it only right and proper to offer young people an analysis of my experience, focusing on the role and the importance of the material in the application of creativity to fashion. At every opportunity I have stressed the fact that for me the concepts of form, color and material constitute a sort of indivisible unity right from the first sketch of an idea for an item of clothing or any other object. At the same time I try to make people understand how, more than ever before, it is the attention paid to the material by the designer, his wish to introduce innovations into it and his taste for experimentation that give sustenance to today's fashion and elegance.

The New Frontier of Creativity
I never tire of saying it: the real frontier of fashion today is to be found in the relationship between the creative intention and research carried out into materials. The success, the fruitful handling of this relationship, give fashion contents of the present and guarantees for the future. Fashion derives its substance and I would even say its physical and tangible existence from the material. And I can say with full confidence that a fundamental part of my creative effort has always taken the form of an innovative and constantly curious approach to material. Over the years cutting-edge processes, increasingly sophisticated treatments and technological experimentation have offered unprecedented possibilities for the utilization of materials. New ones have been created. Procedures, combinations and mixes that would have seemed inconceivable only a few decades ago are now part of reality and of creativity applied to fashion. They constitute a fundamental ingredient of that creativity.
I'm convinced that the importance of the technological input goes beyond its concrete sphere of application and the value of the results obtained, taking on a a significance that I would not hesitate to call cultural. Today's fashion necessarily looks to the future, it thinks in terms of progress, it feeds on advances in technology, after having explored, revived and assimilated all the experiences of style and taste already consolidated in the past.
With direct reference to my experience of the relationship between creativity and material "in the field," I can say with absolute certainty that there is nothing gratuitous about the technological approach, about the impulse to experiment. Research into materials is a necessity. It is research into the substance, the contents, the means which fashion needs in a situation whose characteristics have changed profoundly from those

2.
Gianfranco Ferré
Prêt-à-porter,
P/E 1997

3.
Gianfranco Ferré
Prêt-à-porter,
A/I 1997-1998

4.
Gianfranco Ferré
Prêt-à-porter,
A/I 1997-1998

of the past. Different requirements and habits of life have modified the role of dress and the use of clothing; humanity's attitude toward the environment is different and more conscientious; the way that productive energies are handled to conform to principles like rationalization, profitability and economy is different.

Certainly there is pleasure in experimentation, but it is not sterile virtuosity. Rather it is the play of the imagination and inventiveness that generates the desire to "innovate" in material. It is the pleasure of creativity that tends, naturally, toward the new, toward the original, toward what "does not yet exist." And that therefore has to be created, to be invented.

The Pure Material

Inventing, creating does not signify ignoring the fact that elegance has always relied on noble and precious materials. The world is changing,

just as the relationships between clothing and the body and between humanity and the environment are changing. I cannot think of my style in other terms than those of a great and passionate love for pure materials, as a constant desire to enhance their value and qualities, always proceeding in accordance with the criteria of experimentation, by trial and error, in a process by which the results obtained are gradually brought closer to the desired effect. Silk that is impalpable, substantial or "crisp," in all its variants: taffeta, shantung, organza (fig. 2); wool that is unoiled and smooth or soft and enveloping (fig. 3); leather that is pliable and supple, rendered as soft as cloth, or "forceful" and gritty (fig. 4); jersey that can be as elastic as a second skin or as yielding as the softest of fabrics.

The Material Reinterpreted

It is a question of proper and "improper" uses, unusual and innovative

5.
Gianfranco Ferré
Prêt-à-porter,
A/W 1992-1993

6.
Gianfranco Ferré
Prêt-à-porter,
S/S 1993

7.
Gianfranco Ferré
Prêt-à-porter,
A/W 1994-1995

8.
Gianfranco Ferré
Prêt-à-porter,
A/W 1998-1999

uses of materials that are in reality part of the tradition of clothing. I have updated some materials by using them in a different way from the established rules–which it is right and necessary to know, but also to challenge–for example by demolishing or redrawing the barriers between menswear and women's wear, between day and evening, between formal and informal clothing. Between past and future. Lacquered nylon can be used to construct a fur-bordered jacket that looks sumptuous (fig. 5); crocodile is unusually mixed with black and transparent tulle (fig. 6); raffia combined with gauze turns into bark (fig. 10); the humble cordage used for the rigging of a boat is plaited in a precious and delicate vest (fig. 9); the sturdy leather of English shoes becomes an overcoat; classic camelhair lines the oiled and scoured military trench coat (fig. 7); fur, a timeless object of desire, acquires a futuristic glamour thanks to rubberizing and lacquering (fig. 8); leather, in its "hardest" forms, creates sartorial geometries on the body (fig. 11).

9.
Gianfranco Ferré
Prêt-à-porter,
S/S 1994

10.
Gianfranco Ferré
Prêt-à-porter,
S/S 1993

Speaking of reinterpretation of the material, it is worth taking a look at the importance of the contributions that the industrial world offers ready-to-wear in this area. From industry ready-to-wear takes technological capacities, productive potential and principles of rationalization in manufacturing. My experience has always fitted happily into this framework. In over twenty years of activity I have established a wide range of close and fruitful relationships with the industrial partners that manufacture my collections. I think it would be useful to consider a few examples, with particular reference to GFF, a line conceived with this end in view, approaching the research in a distinctly industrial key, thanks to the structure that Marzotto has set up expressly for its production. Thanks above all to the consolidated know-how of the manufacturing process that is discernible in every GFF collection: the delicate and noble chiffon is crumpled, printed and made to cling to the body (fig. 12); the leather is metalized and laminated, as a sprinkling of

11.
Gianfranco Ferré
Prêt-à-porter,
S/S 1999

12.
GFF,
S/S 1997

13.
GFF,
A/W 1998-1999

14.
GFF
S/S 1999

silver; treated nylon is used for the neo-sartorial suit (fig. 13); the most traditional cotton acquires a state-of-the-art lightness (fig. 14).

The Invented Material
How can material be invented on the threshold of the third millennium, when everything seems to have already been explored, tried out, assimilated? I do not share the fear that there is "no longer anything to invent." My experience and my determination to put every resource and every quality of the material to the test allow me to say that it is possible to "invent" constantly, for example by strengthening the most precious natural fibers by technological means, applying high-definition industrial treatments to traditional materials and coupling profoundly different materials in order to combine their respective qualities.

Inventing material does not mean creating what does not exist, seeking a utopia that negates the physical and concrete reality of the elements

15.
Gianfranco Ferré
Prêt-à-porter,
A/W 1985-1986

16.
Gianfranco Ferré
Prêt-à-porter,
S/S 1987

17.
Gianfranco Ferré
Prêt-à-porter,
A/W 1988-1989

available to the designer. On the contrary, "new material" is born out of the desire to gain an ever deeper understanding of the characteristics and the possibilities of use of what already exists. It is born, above all, out of constant effort, out of a series of trials, out of the small successes of every season. No upheaval, but a constant desire for evolution: usually dull sheepskin, lacquered and made shiny for coats by means of a process used for boots and gardening raincoats (fig. 15); synthetic rubber applied to a Lycra base for swimsuits (fig. 16); lace dipped in rubber for a precious cut-work bolero (fig. 17); the "scuba-diving" suit in shaped Lycra jersey that is as clinging as a wetsuit; "paper fabric" made out of silk that has been crumpled and pleated at high temperature (fig. 20); an unprecedented combination: tulle, studded leather, tailor's stitching (fig. 19); the fisherman's sweater, painted with tar and covered with a light opaque coating; the evening coat in shiny matelassé nylon (fig. 21). If I were to be asked what I would really like to have invented in the field

18.
Prêt-à-porter,
S/S 1999

19.
Gianfranco Ferré
Prêt-à-porter,
A/W 1998-1999

20.
Gianfranco Ferré
Prêt-à-porter,
A/W 1994-1995

21.
Gianfranco Ferré
Prêt-à-porter,
S/S 1997

22.
Gianfranco Ferré
Prêt-à-porter,
A/W 1997-1998

23.
Gianfranco Ferré
Prêt-à-porter,
S/S 1999

24.
Gianfranco Ferré
Prêt-à-porter,
A/W 1994-1995

25.
Gianfranco Ferré
Prêt-à-porter,
A/W 1994-1995

of clothing, I would answer without hesitation: jeans, the true invention in the fashion of our century, a revolution, a symbol, a conquest of freedom and functionality. I didn't invent jeans, but I do "reinvent" them every season, ringing the changes on their basic typology with a range of variations that includes materials of great fascination and refined treatments: denim crumpled to create a paper effect (fig. 21); jeans made of extremely opulent nylon brocade (fig. 22); jeans in a "quasi-*couture*" version with clearly visible tailoring stitches (fig. 23).

Eye-Catching Material: Alchemies and Illusions
I am always happy to associate my work with the concept of alchemy. In reality I believe that for all practical purposes alchemy forms part of it. In my opinion, the term describes in an illuminating way how the creator of fashion can also be the inventor of refined processes for the treatment of materials, in a conscious play of illusions that aims to produce surprising

26.
Gianfranco Ferré
Prêt-à-porter,
A/W 1992-1993

27.
Gianfranco Ferré
Prêt-à-porter,
A/W 1998-1999

28.
Gianfranco Ferré
Prêt-à-porter,
S/S 1999

29.
Gianfranco Ferré
Prêt-à-porter,
A/W 1998-1999

30.
Gianfranco Ferré
Prêt-à-porter,
S/S 1999

effects, to blur the boundary that separates the reality of the material from the pleasure that is provided by the fanciful allusions, impressions and echoes drawn from the most disparate dimensions, and in particular the world of nature and animals. It is a play of fantasy and imagination that finds expression, for instance, in the recourse to the practice of *trompe-l'oeil*, in the judicious use and cunning treatment of materials in order to reproduce the visual effect of others that are completely different in their weight, texture and origin.

It is the pursuit of effect as an intrinsic element of a garment. It is the application of the principle by which "nothing is what it seems." A principle that for me is one of the most fascinating of creative stimuli.

A play of fantasy, as I have said, but also a continual incitement to experimentation, to research, to enhancement of all the potentialities of the material.

In women's wear this is expressed through the use of different materials

31.
Gianfranco Ferré
Prêt-à-porter,
A/W 1998-1999

32.
Gianfranco Ferré
Prêt-à-porter,
A/W 1995-1996

33.
Gianfranco Ferré
Prêt-à-porter,
A/W 1986-1987

34.
Gianfranco Ferré
Prêt-à-porter,
A/W 1997-1998

Gianfranco Ferré

and different weights to reproduce the coat itself, the very skin of animals. Zebra patterns on velvet, pony or chiffon, jaguar spots on lamé and rabbit fur, tiger stripes (fig. 24); faded and softened velvet reproducing the fur of the otter (fig. 25); leather worked in a crochet pattern (fig. 1), densely platted and as wrinkled as the skin of an elephant (fig. 26); "genuine fake" wolfskin obtained from a photographic print (fig. 27); crushed and reconstituted crocodile skin with the scales applied to elastic tulle (fig. 28).

Where menswear is concerned, on the other hand, treated leather and nylon display the same sheen (fig. 29); crumpled cotton is reminiscent of the skin of a reptile (fig. 30); silk is glossy and almost metallic.

Eye-Catching Material: Gleams and Glints

Another important aspect of my passion for alchemy is catching the light and its reflections by playing with the material, creating effects that recall

35.
Gianfranco Ferré
Prêt-à-porter,
A/W 1997-1998

36.
Gianfranco Ferré
Prêt-à-porter,
A/W 1993-1994

Gianfranco Ferré

the splendor of metals, and gold in particular, and of precious stones. A true leitmotiv that runs through my work year after year, collection after collection, in a dimension that reconciles technology with dream. Silver: embroidery and anatomical encrustations on the dress made of tricot and shiny mesh that allows great ease of transport (fig. 34); sieve mesh imprisoning cascades of beads (fig. 32). Gold: matt and "antique" lamé with "spirally-twisted" yarn (metallic spiral), a technique from the 1920s (fig. 33); the barbarous cloak in soft natural leather, gilded and unlined, trimmed with marabou (fig. 35). Gold and copper: the sports jacket bordered with fur, the sumptuous cloak of jacquard taffeta lamé (fig. 36). "Warrior" metal and the "sidereal" gleams of the stars (fig. 31).

37.
Gianfranco Ferré
Prêt-à-porter,
S/S 1999

The Material, the Forms, the Body
Within my creative horizon the role of the human body is fundamental as an immediate referent for every piece of clothing I design. The body with its physicality, its real requirements of movement, its dynamics of relationship with what covers it; the clothing as result of a planned and conscious intervention in the forms, analyzed, composed and put together to attain the desired effect. The process of construction directly involves the material as a primary instrument that makes it possible to create volumes which envelop the body without constraining it, to enhance and sculpt it, to reveal it in a relationship of total symbiosis between the forms of the clothing and those of the body. Thus technological research and the careful processing of the materials in my collections can also be seen as formal research.
Volumes that envelop the body are, for example, the opulent but almost weightless ones of taffeta and tulle that are draped around the waist (fig. 39); a voluptuous but extremely light cone that seems to barely rest on the hips; or again the taffeta that takes on emphasis with movement and wraps the body in a cloud with no weight (fig. 37); the swimsuit as "precursor" of the nude, in stretch tulle-tubular stocking fabric and Lycra (fig. 40); and finally the lightest of evening skirts, made of overlapping

38.
Gianfranco Ferré
Prêt-à-porter,
S/S 1995

39.
Gianfranco Ferré
Prêt-à-porter,
A/W 1994-1995

40.
Gianfranco Ferré
Prêt-à-porter,
S/S 1988

41.
Gianfranco Ferré
Prêt-à-porter,
A/W 1998-1999

42.
Gianfranco Ferré
Prêt-à-porter,
A/W 1994-1995

43.
Gianfranco Ferré
Prêt-à-porter,
S/S 1999

strips of black and white organza. The body is unveiled, instead, by the jumpsuit in elastic organza that coincides perfectly with the body, with pockets that "stand out" (fig. 38); or through strips of knitted fabric that enhance femininity; or again with lacquered trimming cords that decorate the silhouette with arabesques (fig. 41).
The body is sculpted, finally, in the draped evening dresses of casual jersey (fig. 42) or in the irregular strips of cloth that outline the sinuosity of the body in movement (fig. 43).

Cernobbio, September 11, 1999
Fashion Design and Creativity Facing the Challenges of the New Millennium
Fondazione Antonio Ratti. International Textile Forum
Complexity and Turbulence in the Textile Market: Challenges for the New Millennium. Villa d'Este

Preliminary Remarks: Awareness of the Challenges
I cannot help but agree that there is turbulence in today's textile market. Turbulence, or rather inconsistency, the combination of different and contrasting tendencies and phenomena, "movements" that are not always immediately comprehensible and identifiable.
To the fashion designer-manager (the figure that, when all is said and done, plays the creative role today: this is especially true of Italian fashion designers, but a similar situation has developed in the United States and, although somewhat later, in France too), the reasons for and causes of this turbulence are no less clear than to anyone else involved in the fashion scene.
On the one hand there is the saturation of traditional markets for a variety of reasons: demographic stagnation and aging, evolution of mentality and lifestyle and so on. The sector to which the Ferré product belongs–that of uncompromising quality and exclusivity–is not in fact suffering the effects of saturation, but it is clear that the mentality of consumption in the developed countries has changed radically and this is evident in Italy too, where once what counted was the "possession" of objects that indicated power and membership of a particular social class, whereas people are now more interested in the satisfaction of other desires–for travel and vacations, for instance–with a consequent change in the models of life.

Gianfranco Ferré

On the other hand, the globalization of the world economy has led to the opening up of new markets for fashion. Italian fashion, in particular, has made an immediate impact (Ferré has been in Moscow, Warsaw and Bucharest for many seasons, as well as in Beijing and Shanghai and now even in Estonia, Georgia, Kazakhstan and Manchuria). They are markets that are showing a great interest (even in terms of turnover) for our product, that have a strong desire to participate in the changing world and buy quality products, but they have an often unpredictable and risky nature, in part because there is not yet the "cultural" preparation needed to assimilate the type of product.

The globalization of the economy, that is to say of consumption and taste, also involves the globalization of the information that reaches every one without distinction and is growing every day infinitely faster, more incisive and more powerful.

So the strategy has changed: where the fashion designer once worked in secrecy, worried that news of the latest collection would leak out from the atelier too soon, it is now fundamental that information on the value of the label, on its specific qualities, on its new goals is disclosed in quantity, immediately and as widely as possible. The vitality of fashion is now more reliant than ever on information, communication and image. As a consequence, the recognizability of fashion and the label have grown in the eyes of the public. Their desirability has grown too, but from a different perspective than in the past, at least in "mature" markets. People no longer think in terms of status symbols, but of style symbols. Owning and wearing a "fashionable" garment or accessory signifies possessing a certain quality of life, participating in "what is going on," being in some way a protagonist of the ferments and dynamics that are driving events. Possessing a label no longer has value with respect to others, but with respect to oneself. Here the turbulence can be seen as a result of the fluid nature of a situation that is constantly changing and in which what predominates is the desire to assert one's own individuality, in part through clothing.

Last but not least, the turbulence also stems from the assault on the markets by new producing countries, manufacturers of raw materials, yarns, fabrics and finished products, at costs and prices infinitely lower than our own. A tough challenge for our fashion system, for the designers and the big names, for the industrial brands and for the regions where the "superior quality" of Italian clothing is manufactured. A challenge that I believe can be met and overcome by relying precisely on this distinctive heritage, which needs to be reexamined and reinvigorated every day, providing it with contents and coordinates in keeping with the times.

The Emerging Responses of Creativity
Analyzing my experience, I can say with absolute confidence that the responses developed to cope with this turbulence have to a great extent already been turned into business strategies, into concrete objectives of growth. For, while it is true that the fashion designer is not a clairvoyant, it is equally true that "thinking on the fly" is a *sine qua non* for fashion, in creative terms no less than in practical ones. This to some extent is fashion's "mission": reading the signs of the future. Fashion designers, in contrast to what many people believe, do not live in an ivory tower, are not remote from everyday reality. Rather, they read the principal signs of that reality with a sort of "third eye," transforming and sublimating the necessities of life in fashion.

Objectives and Horizons
Individuality, fluidity, freedom: within these coordinates–the coordinates of today's taste and consumption–the focus of fashion design can no longer be exclusively on the clothing itself, but on the clothing that contains the person. The objective moves within the horizons of desire, of patterns of behavior, even of dreams. The aesthetic elaboration that lies at the root of the creative process applied to clothing is now related to potential users, involving the realm of their imagination and feelings.

This is a constant creed that I have been following for years. The creator has to stir the feelings of the clothing's potential user, has to aim for sensations of poetry. Once people bought clothes out of necessity, now they do it for pleasure. We purchase clothes and things because we desire them, because we want them to be ours, on the basis of personal needs, and no longer because they are status symbols.

So the architect of this process is called on to interpret modes of behavior and ways of living and being that pertain to the reality, the society, of our time. With a lead time of at least twelve months, the designer must grasp in advance desires and necessities, moods and aspirations, more or less latent signs of change, reworking his insights into a finished and definitive product with which the end user will be able to identify and feel at ease. It is true that fashion and its product have always been means for the construction of identities and a sense of individuality. But the process of recognition of one's own being and mode of conduct in clothing is based on a new criterion today. It is the criterion of choice, of the free will of the wearer, of his or her independence, of the anti-diktat, of pleasure.

For this whole series of reasons, I have been asserting through my style and my collections for some time that clothing should convey a strong sense of poetry and fantasy, at least in terms of potential. I also hold that at the higher end–the level of luxury ready-to-wear–fashion has to interpret the principle of exceptionality, of the uniqueness that unhesitatingly turns into eccentricity, as absolutely free expression of an individual desire for beauty, diversion and emotion. I myself, after thirty years of working in fashion, want to be seduced when I design a garment, and am the first to be satisfied when I experience this "sense of achievement."

Coherence of Vocabulary and Complex Design

So the product that carries my label has a high "emotional" potential owing to its uniqueness and its versatility, its contents of innovation and exceptionality. Yet it is a product that has always had a strong identity.

An identity that is read as an aggregate of "signs" which are constant over time; in other words of aesthetic creeds that have been repeated and reinforced as genuine leitmotivs, as the lexicon of the Ferré way of dressing, easily recognizable notwithstanding the seasonal variations: formal rigor, precision of the interventions that construct the garment, the constant pleasure of invention, of introducing innovations into the material, the value of consistency in color. A carefully gauged continuity but one that is given concrete expression in formulas and variations that are always new. Variations on a product that are elaborations of modules and models. A vocabulary and an idea of dressing that buyers of the Ferré product have made their own over time and that they will therefore continue to re-create, and to expect from Ferré the designer. Projecting into the future the understanding, the accord that has "constructed" a common ground of reference; a ground on which, almost naturally, the proposals and the stimuli that I offer in my creations establish a relationship with the requirements of "my" consumer.

Coherence of the creative vocabulary, strong identity of the product, customer retention. Three values that in my view "follow" from a common, very sound postulate: a vehicle of expression, a means of identification and for change of the self, clothing has nevertheless to offer guarantees of functional use. To sum up: an object of desire, the item of clothing is and always will be an object of use too. A product that even in a changed and "changing" set of references is interesting, necessary even in the era of non-necessities, and desirable. Because it is conceived in an overall perspective of quality, of duration, of profitability at the level of investment, of distinctiveness. Values that it is the designer's responsibility to turn into reality, to reexamine continually to make sure they do not lose their edge and relevance and to offer to the public in an aesthetically finished form.

This responsibility does not end on the plane of pure design. Or to put it another way, design in fashion today is a continual and complex process. It involves communication, the relationship with the product's end users, its commercial distribution; in short every aspect of the chain whose first link is the original sketch of the garment traced on paper and which concludes on the catwalk where it is shown, on the page of the magazine where its photograph is published, in the window of the boutique where it is offered to the public.

The fashion designer's responsibility as creator and guarantee of this identity of the product, which has to reach the consumer in intact and recognizable form, runs the whole length of the chain. In jest, but with a hint of seriousness, I often say that I am the director of my own shows, the creative manager of my advertising campaigns, the visual merchandiser of my product.

Subdivision of Style

Parallel styles, all fashionable, all different from one another. This has been a fact for at least ten years now. It is the response that creativity has come up with to a reality that is changing, is moving, is growing ever more heterogeneous.

A society, as we have pointed out, of individuals rather than classes or ranks. At the most, a society of "tribes," even in dress, that is characterized by niches of behavior and therefore by niches of consumption.

It is modes of behavior and to an even greater extent occasions that define the consumption of fashion today: the special and unique circumstance, work, daily life, the practice of sport, the pursuit of leisure, vacations. Each of us experiences these occasions, moving from one to the other in accordance with our own rhythms, habits and customs. No longer monolithic, style has been divided into different sectors and covers needs and desires stemming from all these different occasions. The subdivision of style is one of the means by which fashion continues to make sense and have meaning in our lives. And the Ferré style has for many seasons now attained a high degree of subdivision through lines and collections that, while maintaining the consistency of a common aesthetic imprint, are differentiated in their contents and above all in their logic and functions of use. The perspective that prevails is, intentionally, that of complementarity: the exclusivity of luxury of sartorial origin (Gianfranco Ferré) is offered alongside sportswear (Gianfranco Ferré Jeans/Sport), the technological comfort of the casual (GFF) is added to the rigorous naturalness of everyday clothing (Gianfranco Ferré Studio). Each line is split into collections of menswear and women's wear, each with its own "spirit" and character. Just as they move from one occasion, from one circumstance to another in life, potential customers can "move" from one line to another, in some cases even finding them at the same sales outlet. The complex design to which I referred above is therefore a truly all-inclusive design.

Innovation and Production
The birth of Italian ready-to-wear was made possible by a fortunate encounter between fashion designer and industry, between creativity and entrepreneurship. The distinctive character of this liaison is still, I believe, the first ingredient of the Italian "superior quality." The guarantee of its success in the future too. A quality that stems from the constant and very close interaction between the best of whatever the two partners have to offer one another.
Suppleness of structures and flexibility in taking innovative ideas on board, potentialities of production–as well as distribution–that make it possible to think in terms of large numbers, a historical propensity to put the emphasis on quality–owing to the importance of the "human" approach with its roots in craftsmanship that our industry has preserved, but also to the awareness of being able to compete with the global colossi only on the plane of quality. In a nutshell, these are the "treasures" of the Italian manufacturing system on which fashion feeds. In the opposite direction, industry has acquired resources and maturity thanks to the fashion designer. I say this with complete confidence and great pride, thinking of the reality of my relationship with the manufacturers of my

collections, with the big groups like Marzotto and Ittierre no less than with the many prestigious names of smaller companies, quite a few of which are based in the Como region. Constant stimuli to innovate and to improve the product, systematic "injections" of quality, inputs of optimization of the manufacturing process that then become part of the company's overall know-how and, not least, an enhancement of image and increased attention from the media, boosting its overall reputation. The area in which the alliance between fashion design and industry is most fruitful is that of technological experimentation, the result of just that constant, close and daily exchange of stimuli and inputs between the two partners involved to which I have referred. The habit of innovation in the field of material is, fortunately, another strongpoint of our system in which to invest with conviction (and in which I myself have been investing for some time) in order to meet the challenges that the future has in store for us.

Shanghai, April 26, 2001
Creativity and Working Method
Fashion Institute Dong Hua University

1.
Gianfranco Ferré
Prêt-à-porter,
S/S 1993

A virtue and occasional vice. Creativity is one of the fundamental components of the Italian culture and character. It is a sort of flair and at the same time a question of application and precision, a touch of brilliance and a joint effort, just like in the workshops of the Renaissance masters, which have left us all those pictures, statues, frescoes and churches. I often ask myself if we realize to what extent our intelligence still owes a debt to that ancient artisan civilization with whose splendors we are all familiar. A civilization that has led us, through works rich in imagination, spontaneity and individualism, to create what is now known as "the Italian style"; a style of which fashion represents an updating and a variation that moves between spontaneous tradition and design of the present, in a daily rapport between the designer and an industry that has developed a know-how which produces unique results.

"*L'inspiration c'est travailler,*" said Charles Baudelaire, well aware that the momentum comes from working every day, from constant tenacity, from an understanding of technique so deep that you are not trapped by it. Working is the prime form of creativity. A profound truth that I believe I can confirm and share, on the basis of my experience and my daily activity, in the first place through drawing.

It is in a second phase that I draw on my training in geometry and my knowledge of Oriental methods, like origami and the forms of assembly derived from it. At the moment of passing on the models to the factory,

I shift from the sketch to the pattern, breaking the garment down into a series of geometric shapes and developing sections of the details (a sleeve, a buttonhole, a collar): elementary forms that are reworked and placed side by side to give rise to an endless range of solutions. Unique results can be obtained by innovating, experimenting, operating with logic and methodological rigor, paying constant attention to contents and research: a pair of men's pants will always remain a pair of pants, and yet it is possible to invent different pockets, materials and stitching that respect habits and gestures while providing greater comfort.

What count, then, are the "elective affinities" with design. As an architect I hold that fashion is design–defined as the act of transformation that leads from the idea to the object–and that the relationship between architecture and fashion is very close. Apparently architecture is hard and clothes are soft, but even though clothes are soft, I am designing for something *hard* and definitive: the human body.

I construct the silhouette with clarity and precision, enclosing it in geometric forms, in line with my studies that taught me to work within well-established limits. For this reason I never forget that the garment is a flat form that extends over a body: it is two-dimensional, but destined to become three-dimensional. Clothing has its function and significance, but it has to give the person who wears it the possibility of interpreting it. The object-garment comes to life precisely because it is changed by its user. The garment adapts to the body, giving it values and receiving others in turn, without changing its physiognomy, apart from natural deterioration over the years. The garment has a form of its own which can coincide with the body's through the underlining of some parts and the precise allusion of certain details: the waist, for example, is often marked by stiff belts (obis or long strips of black patent leather) or soft ones (organza sashes and georgette scarves). It is a hidden sense of femininity, not the ostentation but the accentuation of certain parts of the body that women have always displayed with naturalness, with a spontaneity that has led me to design clothes and entire collections

2.
Gianfranco Ferré
Prêt-à-porter,
A/W 1992-1993
black India ink
felt-tip pen, red
and gold felt-tip pens
on cardboard

3.
Gianfranco Ferré
Prêt-à-porter,
S/S 1990
black India ink
felt-tip pen and
black wax pastel on
cardboard

around gestures, movements and attitudes: the draping of a hem, the wrapping of a stole around the shoulders, a dress that becomes evanescent in a play of transparences intended to exalt the fluid, essential figure.

A Gianfranco Ferré collection arises out of a formal balance, a golden ratio that my training as an architect has allowed me to transfer into fashion. Here constructive creativity and interpretation meet in a perfect dualism that permeates the whole work. Yet I hold that when it comes to clothing there is little left to invent: what is important rather is to interpret what has already been done with new forms.

From the store of cultural and personal experience gathered in long journeys I derive an imaginary physical and historical landscape through which I "navigate" season by season, following a guiding thread whose broad outlines can be deciphered: India, where I lived in the early seventies; the Japan of courtly dress; the China of simple and elementary forms and the marvelous one of dragons, temples, whorls and figured silks (figs. 2, 4); Eastern teachings and Zen; the great currents of decoration from baroque to romanticism (fig. 3). These are traces that appear during the brief time of the show and that I call 'signs', parts of an ample vocabulary, a lexicon that undergoes variations on the basis of my transformations.

Thus dream, fantasy and inspiration erupt in sudden blazes that illuminate every season with visionary light.

Mexico, Haiti, heat, rum and spices in the summer of 1983. Baroque decorations and motifs in the winter of 1985-86 (fig. 5). A "fictitious" East, as Roland Barthes defined it, in the summer of 1986 (fig. 6) (as the writer observed in *Empire of Signs*, "I can also–though in no way claiming to represent or to analyze reality itself–isolate somewhere in the world (faraway) a certain number of features [...], and out of these features deliberately form a system").

Old fables, languors, 18th-century opulence in the winter of 1989 (fig. 7). The marvels of the Renaissance and baroque mind, the true/false illusion

4.
Gianfranco Ferré
Prêt-à-porter,
A/W 1992-1993

5.
Gianfranco Ferré
Prêt-à-porter,
A/W 1985-1986

6.
Gianfranco Ferré
Prêt-à-porter,
S/S 1986

7.
Gianfranco Ferré
Prêt-à-porter,
A/W 1988-1998

8.
Gianfranco Ferré
Prêt-à-porter,
A/W 1989-1990

9.
Gianfranco Ferré
Prêt-à-porter,
S/S 1989

10.
Gianfranco Ferré
Prêt-à-porter,
A/W 1992-1993

11.
Gianfranco Ferré
Prêt-à-porter,
S/S 1993

12.
Gianfranco Ferré
Prêt-à-porter,
A/W 1992-1993

for the winter of 1990 (fig. 8). A sailor with a romantic nature in love with Hawaii in the summer of 1989 (fig. 9).
And again, the splendors of chinoiserie and the sumptuous red of *The Last Emperor*, in a synthesis of radiant clarity and severity (fig. 10). A green summer in the equatorial forest, shafts of light between the leaves or color as tattooing of the body (figs. 11, 1)

13. Gianfranco Ferré Prêt-à-porter, A/W 1993-1994

I believe firmly in the difference between the sexes and take a clearly separate approach to the problem of preparing lines for them. Designing for men signifies, for me, jotting a spontaneous idea down on paper and then going on to analyze, check and clean it, reducing it to its basic elements. Woman suggests to me intuitions, fantasies, a breath of poetry, while man puts me in mind of reason and a certain transgression, a nonchalance to which feminine composure is less prone.

I show respect for habits in my design and find in the formula of the suit–jacket and pants–the fascinating concept of the uniform. You need a knowledge of the history of men's clothing, but also the capacity to undermine old practices in order to meet new requirements and provide the concreteness typical of the male, to renew the feel of the clothes through the use of unprecedented materials and processes. In my menswear collections I combine the theme of tailoring with the need for suppleness, and express ideas of freedom, the yearning for Africa or India, the taste for sport, the sense of challenge, the desire for adventure: elements that come together and coexist with the principles of the norm and the form, traditional manners, urban living, with the taste and aesthetic stamp of European civilization.

In parallel to the original conception of the clothing, I explore the field of fabrics. I prefer to start out from sensations, explaining to my supplier, the weaver, what sensations I want to obtain when making a certain item out of a particular fabric. We go down the road of experimentation, making use of the most sophisticated processes, on the basis of a very close relationship of collaboration with the manufacturer, who places at my disposal his experience and skill rooted in craftsmanship. The result

14.
Gianfranco Ferré
Prêt-à-porter,
A/W 1989-1990

15.
Gianfranco Ferré
Prêt-à-porter,
S/S 1989

16.
Gianfranco Ferré
Prêt-à-porter,
S/S 1991

17.
Gianfranco Ferré
Prêt-à-porter,
A/W 1989-1990

18.
Gianfranco Ferré
Prêt-à-porter,
A/W 1989-1990

19.
Gianfranco Ferré
Prêt-à-porter,
A/W 1991-1992

20.
Gianfranco Ferré
Prêt-à-porter,
S/S 1985

Gianfranco Ferré

is attained through numerous attempts: thanks to the innovations that come from the application of industrial technology to textiles, I have obtained rubber for swimsuits, macramé knotted out of waxed string (fig. 15), lace immersed in rubber, a stiff and plaited linen that imitates works of joinery, white braid and ribbons resembling openwork stucco (fig. 16), precious moiré, faille and lamé made with "spiral-twisted" yarns, reviving a technique of the twenties. In the collection for winter 1990, intervention in the fabric reaches a peak of virtuosity: the *point d'esprit* veil takes on the transparence and plasticity of the squid (fig. 14); the *gazar* is hot-stamped and assumes the wrinkled appearance of crocodile skin or python scales (figs. 17, 18). I remain a fervent champion of tradition and make use of "pure," classical materials, like shantung or taffeta, moiré or faille, *marocain* given a peach-skin treatment or the richest of brocades, while at the same time falling under the spell of fabrics that have always been linked–for their quality and their comfort– to men's clothing, renovating them and using them in unusual ways: cavalry twill, once used for military greatcoats, the cover coat in wool and cotton and overchecks laid on top of a net of chenille that creates a chevron effect (fig. 19). For color too the principle of necessity holds: it has to be intentional, to have a function and intrinsic significance that justify its use. The basic colors return as constant themes in each collection: white, black, blue and red, alongside natural, more mellow and less absolute tones. Concessions to patterns and bright and clean shades are always deliberate and used in a consistent way that often harks back to my experience of the East, to the unique hues of India (fig. 20). Special consideration is due to one color: gold, with its gleams and glints, sometimes dazzling, sometimes dull and dusty (fig. 21, 22).

If I look at the origins of my creativity, I discover that what I do every day is a mode of operation with ancient roots: a "humanistic" attitude that finds its expressive force in the cult of quality and beauty, the sense of tradition, the love of harmony. My creativity takes on concrete form in the daily confrontation with forms, colors and materials: it is an exercise in rigor and

determination; it is the continual desire to innovate and experiment.
On the threshold of the third millennium personal talent cannot rely on spontaneity alone, and individuality does not mean individualism. The designer is also an entrepreneur. His contribution is made in a complex and varied context, in which an integration is successfully achieved between the human factor and the manufacturing structure: a situation, this last, with highly advanced characteristics, a flexible setup in which the technological component makes it possible to overcome many of the objective limits that once curbed the designer's ambitions.

Italian industry has the merit of adding quality to the handling of the detail, to the use of the material, to the making of the garment. I believe that this ability of the Italian system to organize itself, the speed with which it is capable of analyzing problems and at the same time of focusing on their solution, will permit us, so long as that is what we wish, to carry on being successful.

21.
Gianfranco Ferré
Prêt-à-porter,
A/W 1990-1991

22.
Gianfranco Ferré
Prêt-à-porter,
A/W 1993-1994

Milan, November 17, 2003
The Tailor of Two Cities
Centro Culturale Francese. Palazzo delle Stelline.
Il lunedì degli amici milanesi

1.
Gianfranco Ferré
Prêt-à-porter,
A/W 1988-1989

"Gianfranco Ferré: the tailor of two cities." Out of a sense of impartiality, I am starting this reflection on my French adventure, which lasted over seven years, with a definition that was pinned on me by an American magazine in the years of my creative–as well as physical and geographic– commuting between Milan and Paris.

This certainly meant commuting between two cities, but also between two cultures, two mentalities, two ways of conceiving and proposing elegance. That of Milan, the capital of factory-made *prêt-à-porter*, modern, sober and innovative. A fashion that is the expression of a solid, concrete and discreet city, a bit Calvinistic, a bit withdrawn into itself: into the interiors of its townhouses, into the narrow streets of the center with its still medieval stamp, into the radial layout defined by the Spanish walls.

Paris, by contrast, is a *ville ouverte*, with its broad vistas, its changeable Atlantic sky, its deep-rooted cosmopolitan and multiethnic character. And it is all too easy to say that in Paris fashion means *haute couture*, the hushed allure of the ateliers with their multitude of artisan skills, grandeur, a sense of luxury as an integral part of the national identity and character.

For seven years I was a rather special commuter between these two souls of fashion, so different from one another. An adventure on which it was not very easy to embark, but that turned out to be extraordinary, for my professional and creative development no less than for my human and personal one. The main stumbling-block did not lie so much in logistical problems (the continual shuttling back and forth between Milan and Paris, the automatic doubling of the deadlines, the commitments, the amount of work), as in the bewilderment (to use a decidedly diplomatic expression) caused by the arrival of an "Italian" as stylistic director of an emblem of French style. The most prestigious *maison de couture* in France was a temple of rituals, traditions, codes of conduct and rules, perhaps unwritten but no less hard and fast, no less binding for all that. It was not easy to get used to such a special environment, and yet there were two factors that helped me do it. In the first place my determination, my enthusiasm for the most demanding challenges. I accepted the post after having literally steeped myself in the legendary Dior archives. For weeks on end I studied, analyzed and "breathed" his style. And so I discovered affinities and analogies–and this is the second positive element that made it possible for me to meet the challenge–between my way of understanding and interpreting elegance and that of Monsieur Dior. In the perception, for example, of the svelte and trim female figure even when cloaked in emphatic volumes; in the particular love for noble materials of great beauty; in the sacred care reserved for the cut and all the processes of construction of the garment; in the accent always placed on luxury, understood as uniqueness and exceptionality, as the magic and poetry that have to be conveyed by even the most severe suit for daytime wear. As I have said, my adventure "chez Dior" proved to be an extraordinary opportunity for growth and fulfillment. I never felt the slightest sensation of a split between being Ferré and being Dior. There was never any risk of an overlap between the two aesthetic vocabularies that I found myself interpreting. As I often tell people, in mid-week I left Milan for Paris and was speaking French as soon as I got off the plane.

Having said this, after ten years of *prêt-à-porter*, my approach to the absolute "Frenchness" of the Dior style could only be pragmatic, rooted in design and highly logical. In a word: very Milanese. And very Ferré.

2.
Dior Couture,
A/W 1993-1994

3.
Dior Couture,
S/S 1994

4.
Dior Couture,
A/W 1992-1993

To Dior's *haute couture* I applied techniques borrowed from ready-to-wear, but to an even greater extent I applied the fundamental and modern principle of coherence to the collection, made up of one-off pieces but necessarily bound together by an indispensable thread of logic. I transferred the value and the importance of design into *couture*: the design of the garment as outcome of a reasoned intervention in the forms, even when it was a flowing dress, perhaps a cloud of organza; the design of the collection as a story made up of many impressions and emotions, perhaps different from one another but all immediately traceable back to an identity, to a precise aesthetic and stylistic lexicon. From the opposite perspective, for almost eight years I grew professionally, learning the lesson offered by the atelier on a day-to-day basis: the absolute care taken over the clothing in all its details, the sum of different abilities, all of them exceptional, the maximum of discretion, personalized and unexceptionable service to the clientele. The lesson of the atelier has

5.
Dior Couture,
A/W 1989-1990

6.
Gianfranco Ferré
Prêt-à-porter,
S/S 1999

strengthened in me the conviction that every garment is an entity in its own right, with a story of its own. Every detail, every finishing, every stitch constitutes something unique because it is done *ad hoc* for each individual customer on the basis of her requests and her figure. This state of affairs puts the creator in a position where he is dealing step by step with the professionalism and experience of his collaborators, with the high skills of so many artisans of the kind that only France can still offer and on which the *couturier* has to put his own stamp, giving them a completeness and guiding their work like the conductor of an orchestra on his podium.

So it can be said that mediating between the rituals of the atelier and my aptitude for design lay at the heart of my experience in France. At least in ideal terms, this privileged liaison has certainly not come to an end with the conclusion of my Dior adventure. France, with its culture, its identity and its peculiarities has always, and thus even before the Dior "era," been an integral part of my horizons and my panorama of references. I

love and admire the richness and profundity of its culture. I love its *bon vivre*. I love French cities, the sense of the city as a single "entity" and not as a combination of separate realities. A sense that is perhaps lacking in our cities, notwithstanding their beauty, along with the political and administrative courage needed for the implementation of significant and farsighted interventions that will ensure quality of life and development in the future. I love the French understanding of luxury and way of proposing it, undoubtedly more emphatic than the Italian one, more institutionalized and indisputably better promoted than ours.

7.
Gianfranco Ferré
Prêt-à-porter,
A/W 2002-2003

8.
Gianfranco Ferré
Prêt-à-porter,
S/S 2000

9.
Gianfranco Ferré
Alta Moda,
A/W 1988-1989

10.
Dior Couture,
A/W 1989-1990

11.
Dior Couture,
A/W 1992-1993

Istanbul, December 8, 2006
Exotic Inspirations
International Herald Tribune. Luxury Conference 2006.
The Ritz Carlton Hotel

1.
Gianfranco Ferré
Prêt-à-porter,
S/S 1989

The Global Intelligence of Fashion
I think the revisiting of periods and places, the mixing of past and future, of East and West, is a key component of the "global intelligence" of fashion. The need to ignore time limits and spatial boundaries in order to find the data, stimuli and sensations out of which to construct its messages is part of fashion's genetic makeup. The luxury of the Italian Renaissance courts, for example, fascinated every corner of the known world, while the elegance of Napoleon's court set the standard in St. Petersburg just as in Vienna or London. For hundreds of years European tailors and dressmakers have stolen ideas (and not just ideas) from other continents, letting their imagination run wild in *chinoiseries*, the charms of India, colonial influences. Not to speak of the spell of mystery, opulence and incomparable refinement that the Ottoman world cast over the whole of Europe for centuries and centuries. If we look at creativity applied to fashion, the comparison and mixing of different cultures has always been a source of enrichment and originality. In many cases fashion has been able to serve as the vehicle for the recovery and reutilization of certain expressions foreign to Western civilization that would otherwise have been doomed to oblivion or dismissed as primitive curiosities.
I'm certain that fashion will go on feeding on emotions and impressions of very different origins, periods and cultural backgrounds. There is not, in this sense, a goal to be reached. Instead there is a process of constant

evolution that is at once a reworking of previous experiences and a constant search for the new.

Fashion without Borders
This is the dimension in which is set my deep and constant passion for different cultures and for the "disparate" horizons that can be evoked by stories, by books, by films. Particularly important here are my journeys, the real ones or the ones I have made in my imagination. It could be said that my favorite journey is the one that starts out from a peculiar interaction between experience of the real world and the world I have only dreamed. It is an interaction from which come the sensory data, dreams, visions, desires and emotions that are the lifeblood of my creativity. "The repeated references to distant cultures help to explain the profound diversity of my style. Seduced by that taste for asymmetry which is the great spatial intuition of the Japanese, by the fluid, incessant harmony of the Far East or by the pure emphasis of India, with the enormous skirts, puffed sleeves and rigid bodices of Rajasthan, by gigantisms, energetic tonalities and eccentric touches. From bust to waist run ornaments and well-supported flounces. Collars burst open to become window-frames giving proportion to the figure or are reduced to the minimum, composing a lexicon in which the signs can be interpreted as people wish, since there is no one way of understanding things".[1] Recounting my travels in the collections in no way reflects a desire to escape from the reality in which we live. On the contrary, all the "exotic" inspirations that are to be found in them can be related to an all-embracing project that has meaning here and now, not in the mysterious jungles of Borneo or the rainforest of Amazonia.

2.
Gianfranco Ferré
Prêt-à-porter,
S/S 1991

3.
Gianfranco Ferré
Prêt-à-porter,
S/S 2002

The Lesson of the East
I think I can say that without the East my style would have been profoundly different. India, for instance, gave me an enthusiasm for that whole range of colors which lie between yellow, red and fuchsia: the orangey, sunny, bright tints that Indian women often choose for their

saris because they are the cheapest and easiest to obtain through dyeing, but that made a lasting impression on my imagination for the sense of vitality, passion and even opulence that they convey.

The sari itself gave me a great lesson in elegance: absolute simplicity and a thousand shades of color; a thousand ways of draping it, every fold with a significance of its own in an immediate and natural relationship with the body in movement. Observing Indian women draped in their saris–as well as Chinese women in their loose jackets and pants or Laotian and Vietnamese women in their sarongs–I have seen that they are able to carry out the most humble and backbreaking tasks while preserving an absolutely regal appearance.

This taught me, among other things, what I call "the sense of the body," that is to say its physicality and its movements as elements of reference to which I give absolute priority in the process of constructing clothing. The lesson of the East has allowed me to readjust the principle of luxury and

opulence, not by turning my back on them, but by setting out instead to eliminate the superfluous, the redundant, the frills.

The Thousand Souls of India

Knowing and loving the place as deeply as I do, I am aware that India has a thousand faces and a thousand souls. Its history and its reality are so complex that they appear unfathomable and uncharted, and thus offer constant surprises. India is always capable of astonishing, bewitching and fascinating you, thanks not just to its age-old glories and refinements, but also to the high-tech of Bangalore and the virtual splendors of Bollywood. For me the subcontinent is a magical story that never fails to cast its spell on me, and which I propose in my designs through paraphrases and citations. In this enthusiastic exploration, I have always tried to show just how much there is in the ancient soul of this amazing country that is pure and strong, energetic and free, modern and stimulating (figs 2, 3).

4.
Gianfranco Ferré
Prêt-à-porter,
A/W 1992-1993

5.
Gianfranco Ferré
Prêt-à-porter,
A/W 1990-1991

6.
Gianfranco Ferré
Prêt-à-porter,
A/W 1981-1982

7.
Gianfranco Ferré
Prêt-à-porter,
S/S 2003

The China of Raise the Red Lanterns

My China is the one that remains in my distant but still clear recollections of a visit to Canton at the height of the Cultural Revolution, but above all in the memories of books, in the fables and stories that the West, constantly fascinated by an eternal, enigmatic and extremely refined civilization, has always produced in abundance.

It is a China seen through a sort of lens that filters sentiments, impressions and discoveries. In this vision predominates, for example, the gleam of gold, that metal of incorruptible beauty, emblem of power and wealth. Gold is irresistible and absolute, and brightens up clothing: it can be glittering and dazzling or dull and dusty, combined with the red of lacquers, the green of jade, the blue of lapis lazuli and woven into the sumptuous weaves of brocade and damask. And it becomes the emblem of a China that hardly exists any longer, but is still an absolute empire of signs (figs. 4, 5).

Japan, Graceful Warrior

Japan has given me a special "inspiration": the development of complex forms out of simple ones, rather along the lines of origami.
Many of the other big and small impressions that have long left a mark on my imagination and my fantasy are "Japanese." The almost sacred gestural expressiveness, for example, of the country's theater and the real one of its everyday life: measured, always elegant, never flamboyant, full of grace and composure. Or the pride of feudal Japan, of a world of warriors, with its rituals, its codes of conduct and expression: a dimension that in every aspect conveys a sense of beauty that is at once daunting and exceptionally refined (figs. 6, 7).

Other Horizons: Out of Africa
Africa is a world that I have visited only in my imagination and that, perhaps for this very reason, is able to move me enormously. I am always deeply impressed

8.
Gianfranco Ferré
Prêt-à-porter,
S/S 2001

9.
Gianfranco Ferré
Prêt-à-porter,
S/S 2001

10.
Gianfranco Ferré
Prêt-à-porter,
S/S 1994

by pictures of African women, beautiful in an ancestral, mysterious, solemn manner. Capturing the nature of their elegance is like trying of decipher the deepest meaning of femininity. Playing with dreams and with sensations, I have transformed the luxury of warriors, the opulence of tribes and the magnificence of the primitive into marks of elegance for our own time. Naturally I have not limited myself to pure citation: what have come out of "my" Africa are emotions and impressions, but also the logic and intention of research and the modern sense of the body. I have allowed a certain opulence to express all its symbolic richness: the style of a piece of jewelry, the shade of a fabric, the draping of a garment's hem. I have tried to worm out of this mysterious continent the secret of the sublime energy of its elegance, the profundity of its soul and above all its extraordinary ability to create splendors and treasures, starting out almost always from elementary, even "poor" materials in the awareness of how little African luxury has to do with ostentation, and how much it is instead a story of pride, dignity, majesty and beauty (figs. 9, 10).

A Thousand and One Nights
Western fashion has always fallen under the intense, diverse and enchanting spell of the Near East, stealing from it ideas and impressions, styles, processes and decorations. I myself, for example, have borrowed some themes of the region's cabinetmaking, translating them into embroidery, cutwork and inlays. I have also played around with typically Middle Eastern modes of dress, like the caftan or the burnoose (at once elegant and very simple), enriching them with embroidery, applications and trimmings so as to turn them into sumptuous evening dresses. It's almost too easy to say that, in my imagination too, Turkey, or rather the Ottoman Istanbul of mosques, of minarets, of sumptuous and secret palaces, represents the perfect and ideal backdrop to a vision that can only approximately be called Oriental. For it is the place where, in reality, the East is already West and the West succumbs to the fascination of the East.

11.
Gianfranco Ferré
Prêt-à-porter,
S/S 2005

12.
Gianfranco Ferré
Prêt-à-porter,
A/W 1989-1990

13.
Gianfranco Ferré
Prêt-à-porter,
A/W 1989-1990

14.
Gianfranco Ferré
Prêt-à-porter,
S/S 1993

In the Jungle: from Africa to Amazonia

As a modern alchemist, I have used technology to evoke the natural world of the jungle, dreaming up magical spells and devices, imagining a green summer in the equatorial forest with shafts of light between the leaves and dazzling visions of animals. Between truth and illusion I have sought surprising materials with an echo of the fabulous: tarnished and dipped gold and other metals, cascades of primitive jewelry made out of very light balsa, wooden plaques that adorn the body. But the jungle also enchants me with the wild beauty of the fauna that throngs it. For me nothing is more intriguing than the richness offered by the coats of animals: those of the felines, above all, but also of the zebra or the giraffe, of the elephant or the alligator. And nothing is more intriguing than the alchemical process which reproduces this prodigious kaleidoscope: the scales of the alligator represented by embroidery and applications, the wrinkled skin of the elephant recreated on crêpe, the fur of the leopard,

the jaguar, the cheetah, printed on the most feminine and sexy of fabrics, from voile to tulle and chiffon (figs. 11, 12, 13, 14).

México Hermoso
If I think of the Mexican lexicon, I think of the joyful and radiant femininity of the country's women, of the intense light of midday reflected from the façades of colonial buildings and magnificent cathedrals. In a logic that sees white not just and not so much as a color, but as a declaration of vitality. But Mexican vitality is not at all monotone. It can be kaleidoscopic, vibrating, for example, in the hues of the rocks and the wild flowers of the Sierra: blood red, vermilion. It vibrates too in the charming gesture with which the women wrap themselves in their mantillas to protect themselves from the evening breeze. It vibrates above all in the opulence, in the almost ritual glories of certain pieces of lace or embroidery, of tinkling bracelets, of gleaming chains that call to mind the sacred jewelry of the *Virgen de Guadalupe* (figs. 15, 16).

Pampas & Tango Glamour

Argentina is for me the symbol of a romantic, perhaps rather severe but poignant and intense femininity. A femininity that lives and vibrates in the echoes of a bustling metropolis, as well as in the allusions to seemingly endless landscapes, lit by clear southern skies.

Thinking of this femininity, I have reworked in a glamorous key the mantles that Argentineans used to wear when riding on the pampas. I have designed boots that recall the gaucho's *botas de potro*, skirts that grow long and full, with dense and pleated ?flounces? that seem to dance with the wearer's movement, creating an irresistible swishing sound. And from under their hems peeps the tapered form of the tango shoe, with its faint and enticing pitter-patter fading into the *porteño* night (figs. 17, 18).

On the Sea: from Hawaii to Punta del Este

You can't help falling in love with the sea of the tropics. With its languor and its gentleness. With the sensuality and freedom of Hawaiian or Polynesian beaches. With the exotic flowers woven into garlands that become the most precious and inviting of ornaments. With straw skirts– obviously reinvented by technological means–that sway on the hips, perpetuating a timeless ritual of seduction.

From the Pacific to the Atlantic: decidedly less languid, the ocean is also a sense of freshness and openness. It is the dimension of invigorating relaxation that I have associated with an imaginary Atlantic crossing aboard a cutter that is sailing under full canvas toward Punta del Este. It is the dimension in which everything is impetus and speed, in which bodies are supple, legs leap freely, the proportions of the clothes are reduced, the colors are basic and essential (fig. 1).

NOTE

[1] Gianfranco Ferré, "The Course of Design," lecture, International Design Conference. Aspen, June 17, 1989.

15.
Gianfranco Ferré
Prêt-à-porter,
S/S 2004

16.
Gianfranco Ferré
Prêt-à-porter,
S/S 2006

17.
Gianfranco Ferré
Prêt-à-porter,
S/S 2006

18.
Gianfranco Ferré
Prêt-à-porter,
A/W 2005-2006

Milan, June 14, 2007

The Forms of Emotion. Giving Form to Feelings
Milan Polytechnic. School of Design
Graduate course in Fashion Design

1.
Gianfranco Ferré
Prêt-à-porter,
A/W 1994-1995

We prefer to stand with our feet firmly on the ground, but with our head among the stars.
(MIES VAN DER ROHE)

A declaration of intent. Reason or emotion?
Creating an item of clothing is undoubtedly an operation of the imagination, a manifestation of feeling and intuition. It is an emotional process that presupposes impulse and inventiveness, that brings into play suggestions, sensations, impressions.
Yet the methodological approach is an indispensable aspect of creative activity. The emotional and sensory input has to be rationalized, analyzed, codified and brought within a perspective of design.
Thus creating a garment means knowing how to dream rationally.

Anyone can have ideas, imagination, but this has no value if you do not know how to construct the garment. (HUBERT DE GIVENCHY)

THE FIRST POSTULATE

In principle there is form because every garment is, in the first place, a formal design. An indispensable part of this design process is the conception of the clothing as the result of a planned and conscious intervention in forms. In clothing, producing an emotional effect means composing forms and taking them apart, analyzing and understanding them, developing and interpreting them.

THE SECOND POSTULATE

The necessary form is that of the human body, with its physicality, its real requirements of movement, its dynamics of relationship with what covers it and what surrounds it.
Every design of an item of clothing starts out, in fact, from a two-dimensional phase–that of the design "fixed" on paper in the form of a drawing–but implies from the outset a confrontation with the three-dimensionality of the human figure. The confrontation with this "necessary" form confers identity, substance and logic on the garment.

2.
Gianfranco Ferré
prêt-à-porter
S/S 1999
black India ink
felt-tip pen and
black wax pastel on
cardboard

3.
Gianfranco Ferré
Alta moda
A/W 1987-1988
black India ink
felt-tip pen, black
felt-tip pen
on cardboard

Gianfranco Ferré

4.
Gianfranco Ferré
prêt-à-porter
A/W 1982-1983,
black India ink
felt-tip pen, black
and royal blue felt-tip
pens on cardboard

5.
Gianfranco Ferré
Prêt-à-porter,
S/S 2004

6.
Gianfranco Ferré
Prêt-à-porter,
S/S 2004

This is the prerequisite for clothing to be able to perform its function as an "object of use," that is to say a product tailored to the reality of life.

THE THIRD POSTULATE

Form has a substance, which is the material. The process of construction of the garment directly involves the material and depends on it. The material is the primary instrument that allows the creation of forms and volumes, the gauging of lines and proportions. Technological research, experimentation and innovation in materials can also be seen as formal research. A dynamic relationship with the material is the *sine qua non* for the success of the formal design.

THE DYNAMICS OF THE DESIGN PROCESS

Elaborating

As has already been said, creating an article of clothing means embarking on a process of formal construction. The logic that underlies this process is that of the elaboration of simple geometric forms into complex ones that are projected into three dimensions.
As in every design, the first, necessary step in the process of formal elaboration is the "definition" of the forms themselves in the guise of a sketch. The geometric connotations of the forms that will characterize the clothing can easily be grasped in the sketch (figs. 2, 3, 4, 5, 6).

Simplifying

In many cases the process of formal elaboration of the garment takes on the character of a quest for linearity. This quest leads to the elimination

7.
Gianfranco Ferré
Prêt-à-porter,
S/S 1997
black India ink
felt-tip pen, brown
and black wax
pastel on cardboard

8.
Gianfranco Ferré
Prêt-à-porter,
A/W 1997-1998
black India ink
felt-tip pen, black
wax pastel on
cardboard

9.
Gianfranco Ferré
Prêt-à-porter, S/S
1996

10.
Gianfranco Ferré
Prêt-à-porter, A/W
2007-2008

11.
Gianfranco Ferré
Prêt-à-porter,
A/I 1993-1994,
black India ink
felt-tip pen, on paper

12.
Gianfranco Ferré
Prêt-à-porter,
A/I 1993-1994

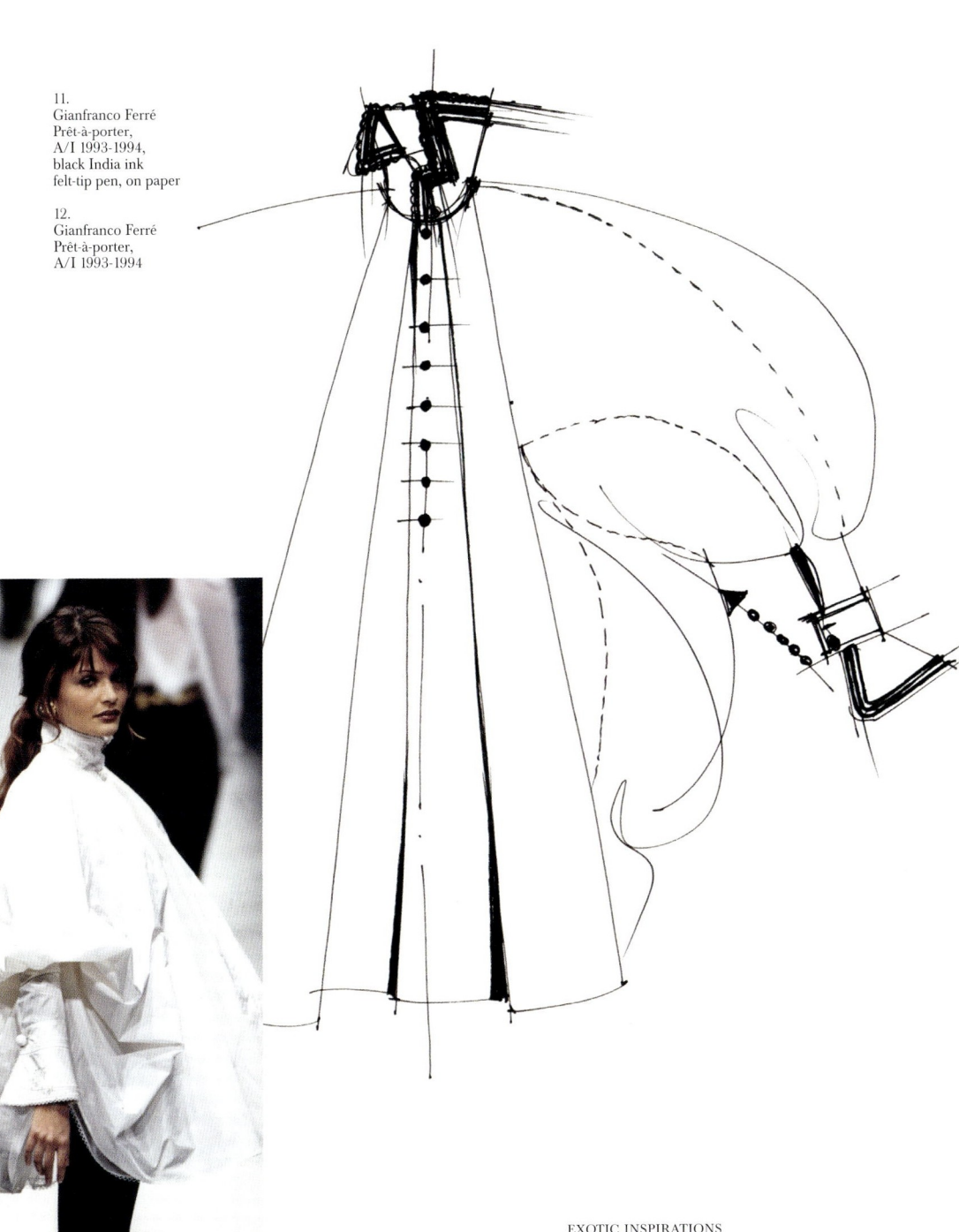

EXOTIC INSPIRATIONS

of all superfluity and the result is an impression of clarity and rigor. The values of essentiality do not apply exclusively to daywear, but to eveningwear too, in a general perspective of "ease" that governs the approach to dress today.
In the presence of an absolute linearity of form, therefore, the garment's potential for glamour often stems from the preciosity of the decoration (figs. 7, 8, 9, 10).

Emphasizing
Yet the approach to the forms of the clothing cannot disregard the qualities of magic and dream that it has always been called on to express. So the design of the forms becomes a search for emphasis, opulence and grandeur. "Playing around" with emphasis signifies in the first place conceiving prominent, sumptuous and enveloping volumes. Even prominent volumes are necessarily derived from the elaboration

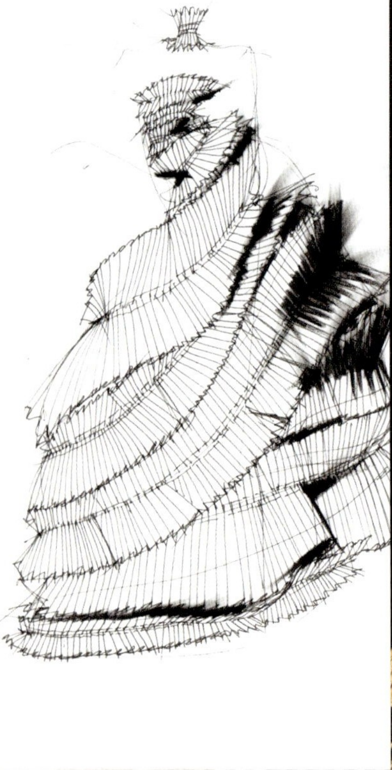

13.
Gianfranco Ferré
Prêt-à-porter,
A/W 2000-2001,
matita, pennarello
nero china e pastello
a cera nero su
cartoncino

14.
Gianfranco Ferré
Prêt-à-porter,
A/W 2005-2006

15.
Gianfranco Ferré
Prêt-à-porter,
S/S 1999, pennarello
nero china, pastello
cera nero e pastello
ocra su cartoncino

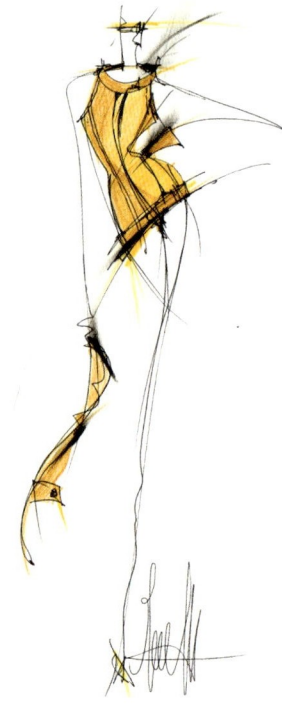

16.
Gianfranco Ferré
Prêt-à-porter,
S/S 1995

17.
Gianfranco Ferré
Alta moda
A/W 1986
pencil, black felt-tip pen, pink felt-tip pen on paper

18.
Gianfranco Ferré
Prêt-à-porter,
A/W 1994-1995

of elementary forms, in a logic that has to take account of the needs of movement and thus of wearability, something which also applies to the most magnificent of garments (figs. 11, 12, 13, 14).

Reducing
The search for essentiality also leads to a reduction of the proportions and dimensions of the garment itself, or of some parts of it. The immediate result is an accentuation of the ease with which the clothing can be worn.
But a perhaps even more important result is the redefinition of the "boundaries" between different types of clothing: the jacket turns into a bolero, the dress into a blouse, pants are drastically cut down into shorts, the blouse becomes a top, the coat whose sleeves stop at the elbow acquires a new identity (figs. 15, 16).

Taking Apart

The interplay of forms can also find expression in the "breakdown" of the garment itself, that is to say in the elimination of some parts of it. The aim behind this process is the search for effect as the characterizing value of clothing. So, the smock can "lose" its bodice while retaining sumptuous sleeves or the most rigorous tuxedo jacket can lose its sleeves, leaving the arms bare (figs. 17, 18, 1).

Readjusting

In the search for effect, the intrinsic harmony of the garment can be reconsidered. It is sufficient to place the accent on a detail or amplify the dimensions and proportions of one part of the item of clothing, creating elements that are deliberately "out of proportion." Collars, cuffs and bows of "exaggerated" size can turn the simplest of garments into something complete, unique and special. They become the essence of

19.
Gianfranco Ferré
Prêt-à-porter,
A/W 1986-1987,
pencil, black India
ink felt-tip pen and black
and pink felt-tip pens
on cardboard

20.
Gianfranco Ferré
Prêt-à-porter,
A/W 1988-1989,
pencil, black, blue,
red and pink felt-tip
pens on cardboard

21.
Gianfranco Ferré
Prêt-à-porter,
A/W 2004-2005

22.
Gianfranco Ferré
Prêt-à-porter,
A/W 2001-2002

23.
Gianfranco Ferré
Prêt-à-porter,
S/S 2000,
black India ink
felt-tip pen, black
felt-tip
pen on cardboard

24.
Gianfranco Ferré
Prêt-à-porter,
S/S 1999

the clothing and, according to the logic of *pars pro toto*, the garment itself (figs. 19, 20, 21, 22).

Eliminating

The garment can even "lack" a form of its own in order to take on completely that of the body. This result is obtained by working on the material, in other words by emphasizing its ability to cling or relying solely on its cut. In this case the clothing "sculpts" the body, while the body "constructs" the clothing. The garment ceases to be "superstructure" and becomes essence. It is a return to primary form (figs. 23, 24). Many people have described my clothes as works of "textile architecture." I like the definition. It clearly conveys the idea of what clothing is for me: the result of an encounter between form and material, "guided" by the designer's hand. I would not choose to use any other definitions. I would simply add this: my clothes are works of textile architecture conceived for the body. Which the body brings to life.

Biography

Gianfranco Ferré was born at Legnano (Milan), on August 15, 1944.
After attending high school, he enrolled in the Department of Architecture at Milan Polytechnic, graduating in 1969 with a thesis on the *Methodology of the Approach to Composition* under Franco Albini.
He made his debut in the fashion world by chance in the same period: Ferré designed jewelry and accessories that he gave to his friends and fellow students. His creations were noticed by Rosy Biffi, proprietor of a groundbreaking boutique who told Ileana Pareto Spinola and Anne Sophie Benazzo about them: won over by the ingeniousness of these objects which were still made by hand, they put them in their showroom and offered them to buyers. Attracting the attention of fashion editors (Anna Piaggi and Anna Riva were the first) almost by chance, photographs of them were published in magazines: in 1971 one of the accessories appeared on the cover of *Arianna* and then in *Grazia, Linea Italiana*... A debut that was already a success, with the help of Camilla Cederna, who wrote about them in the column "Il lato debole" she ran in the weekly *L'Espresso*.
In 1973 Gianfranco Ferré made the first of many journeys to India, where he worked for long periods up until 1977: for a Genoese manufacturer, San Giorgio Impermeabili, owned by the Borelli family, he designed the *Ketch* collection and had it produced locally. This gave him the opportunity to visit every part of the country, studying its handicrafts and productive potentialities, an activity he carried out in part on behalf of the Indian government. Ferré was literally entranced by India, where he began to explore his creativity: India, a fundamental lesson in life, made up of emotions and sensations linked to the colors, scents and forms that he was to transfer into his collections, through his own particular way of remembering them.

In the same years, during the periods he spent in Italy, he maintained relationships of collaboration on the design of accessories with established names like Walter Albini and Christiane Bailly and worked as an advisor to manufacturers of knitwear and swimwear. The latter was shown for the first time at MareModa Capri, where it won him a prize that was the first in a long series of awards.

In 1974 he designed and showed his first collections of *prêt-à-porter*: *Courlande* and *Baila*, the latter commissioned from him by Franco Mattioli, the Bolognese entrepreneur with whom he would go into partnership in 1978.

It was in May 1978 that he founded the Gianfranco Ferré company, with its head office first on Via San Damiano and then on Via della Spiga. In October of the same year he staged his first show of women's ready-to-wear at the Hotel Principe di Savoia in Milan.

He followed up the launch of his line of menswear in 1982, and the creation of a range of accessories and other products made under license by numerous leading companies in their respective categories, with a venture into the world of high fashion in 1986, holding shows in Rome for six seasons.

In 1983 he helped to draw up the teaching program of the newly founded Domus Academy, a postgraduate school of design, design management and fashion design where he ran the course of clothing design until 1989: analysis of the problems involved in the design of garments and its connections with changes in fashion, and of the design process itself.

May 1989 saw the beginning of his extraordinary adventure in the name of Christian Dior: Gianfranco Ferré was appointed artistic director of the women's *haute couture*, *prêt-à-porter* and *fourrure* lines at the most prestigious and historic house in French high fashion. He was reappointed to his post at Dior in 1993 and stayed until 1996.

In the fall of 1998, the 20th anniversary of the foundation of his label was marked by a series of events that would prove decisive for the future of the company, culminating with the opening of a new headquarters in Milan, the former Gondrand Building on Via Pontaccio, completely renovated to a design by Marco Zanuso.

In 2002 the Gianfranco Ferré company was taken over by Tonino Perna's IT Holding and Gianfranco Ferré became its artistic director.

In March 2007 he was elected president of the Accademia di Brera.

On June 17, 2007, Gianfranco Ferré died following a brain hemorrhage.

Essential Bibliography

Writings on Gianfranco Ferré

ALFONSI, MARIA VITTORIA, *Gianfranco Ferré. L'architetto stilista.* Milan: Baldini Castoldi Dalai Editore, 2008.

ALFONSI, MARIA VITTORIA, *Questo è il made in Italy ovvero la moda dietro la vetrina.* Milan: GEI, 1986, pp. 360-64.

B'96. Il tempo e la moda. Milan, Skira, 1996, pp. 394-9.

BAUDOT, FRANÇOIS, *A Century of Fashion.* London: Thames & Hudson, 1999, pp. 251, 254, 354-5.

BIANCHINO, GLORIA; QUINTAVALLE, ARTURO CARLO, *Moda. Dalla fiaba al design. Italia 1951-1989.* Novara: De Agostini, 1989, pp. 137, 140, 153, 156, 170, 226-39.

BINGHAM, NEIL, *The New Boutique: Fashion and Design.* London: Merrell Publishers, 2005.

BOBBIONI, MARIA PIA, "Gianfranco Ferré," in *Conseguenze impreviste. Moda.* Florence: Electa, 1982, pp. 35-40.

BOCCA, NICOLETTA; CATALDI GALLO, MARZIA, "Gianfranco Ferré," in *La moda italiana. Dall'antimoda allo stilismo*, edited by Grazietta Butazzi and Alessandra Mottola Molfino. Milan, Electa, 1987, pp. 134-42.

BUTAZZI, GRAZIETTA; MOTTOLA MOLFINO, ALESSANDRA (eds.), *La moda italiana. Dall'antimoda allo stilismo*. Milan: Electa, 1987, pp. 22-3, 31, 177, 187.

CARLONI, MARIA VITTORIA, "Milano, laboratorio dell''Italian Style,'" in *1951-2001. Made in Italy?*. Milan: Skira, 2001, pp. 145-7.

CHENOUNE, FARID. *Dior*. Paris, Editions Assouline, 2007.

COLAIACOMO, PAOLA; FRISA, MARIA LUISA, "Some Random Notes on Italian Fashion. The Fashion of Postmodernism," in DURLAND SPILKER, KAYE; SADAKO TAKEDA, SHARON, *Breaking the Mode: Contemporary Fashion from the Permanent Collection of the Los Angeles Museum of Art*. Milan, Skira, 2007.

Dictionnaire international de la mode, edited by Bruno Remaury and Lydia Kamitsis. Paris, Editions du Régard, 1994-2004, pp. 237-8.

Dizionario della Moda, edited by Guido Vergani. Milan: Baldini Castoldi Dalai Editore, 2000.

DURLAND SPILKER, KAYE; SADAKO TAKEDA, SHARON, *Contro moda. La moda contemporanea della collezione permanente del Los Angeles County Museum of Art*. Milan, Skira, 2007, pp. 152-3.

Ferré. Milan: Edizioni Condé Nast, 1993 (supplement to *Vogue Italia*, no. 510, February).

FERRÉ, GIUSI, *Mazza Samuele, Gianfranco Ferré*. Milan: Leonardo Arte, 1998.

FERRÉ, GIUSI (ed.), *Gianfranco Ferré. Itinerario*. Milan: Leonardo Arte, 1999.

FERRI, EDGARDA, *Ferré*. Milan: Longanesi & C., 1995.

GIACOMONI, SILVIA, *L'Italia della moda*. Milan: Mazzotta, 1984, pp. 106-9.

GIANNELLI BUSS, CHIARA, "Gianfranco Ferré," in *La moda italiana. Dall'antimoda allo stilismo*, edited by Grazietta Butazzi and Alessandra Mottola Molfino. Milan: Electa, 1987, pp. 251-5.

GIANNELLI BUSS, CHIARA, "Lo stilismo nella moda maschile," in *La moda italiana. Dall'antimoda allo stilismo*, cit., pp. 237, 240, 244.

GIORDANI ARAGNO, BONIZZA, "?Italian Fashion?," in SEELING, CHARLOTTE, *Fashion: The Century of the Designer. 1900-1999.* Cologne: Konemann, 2000.

GIORDANI ARAGNO, BONIZZA, "Lo specchio dell'atelier," in *La moda italiana. Le origini dell'alta moda e la maglieria*, edited by Gloria Bianchino, Grazietta Butazzi, Alessandra Mottola Molfino and Arturo Carlo Quintavalle. Milan: Electa, 1987, p. 104.

GIORDANI ARAGNO, BONIZZA (ed.), *Moda Italia.* Milan: Editoriale Domus, 1988, pp. 96-101.

HARVEY, ANNA, *Fashion: Great Designers Talking.* London: MQ Publications, 1998.

Japonism in Fashion. Tokyo: The Kyoto Costume Institute, 1996, pp. 168, 190.

MASSAI, ELISA; LOMBARDI, P, "L'industria della maglieria nell'alta moda and nella moda pronta dal 1950 al 1980," in *La moda italiana. Le origini dell'alta moda e la maglieria*, cit., pp. 264, 271.

MCDOWELL, COLIN, *Fashion Today.* London: Phaidon Press, 2000, pp. 100-101, 165-6.

MESSINA, RIETTA, "L'abbigliamento femminile italiano: un prodotto industriale di successo," in cit., p. 31.

MORINI, ENRICA. *Storia della Moda XVIII-XX secolo.* Milan: Skira, 2000.

MORINI, ENRICA; BOCCA, NICOLETTA, "Lo stilismo nella moda femminile," in *La moda italiana. Dall'antimoda allo stilismo*, cit., pp. 90, 93.

MULASSANO, ADRIANA, *I Mass Moda. Fatti e personaggi dell'Italian look.* Milan: G. Spinelli & C., 1979, pp. 188-195.

POCHNA, MARIE-FRANCE, *Dior.* Paris: Editions Assouline, 1996.

POCHNA, MARIE-FRANCE, *Dior.* Florence: Octavo Franco Cantini Editore, 1997.

PUPPA, DANIELA, "Mutazioni stagionali 1," in *Domus Moda*, May 1981, pp. 44-9.

REINHOLD, ELKE, "?From the Drawing to the Finished Garment?," in SEELING, CHARLOTTE, op. cit., p. 301.

ROCCA, FEDERICO, *Embroidery Italian fashion: Il ricamo nella moda italiana.* Bologna: Damiani, n.d. (but 2006), pp. 174-7, 255-7.

SOLI, PIA, *Il genio antipatico. Creatività e tecnologia della moda italiana 1951-1983.* Milan: Mondadori, 1984.

SOLI, PIA; SALAROLI, SERGIO, *Moda. L'immagine coordinata/ Corporate Identity.* Bologna: Zanichelli, 1990, pp. 110-37.

SOLLAZZO, LUCIA, *Tutti in vetrina. Il romanzo della moda italiana.* Milan: Longanesi & C., 1996, pp. 103-16.

Writings by Gianfranco Ferré

FERRÉ, GIANFRANCO, *A un giovane stilista.* Milan: Pratiche Editrice, 1996.

FERRÉ, GIANFRANCO, *Lettre à un jeune couturier.* Paris: Editions Ballard, 1995.

FERRÉ, GIANFRANCO; TADINI, EMILIO, "L'abito e il corpo. Il corpo e la figura," in *La moda italiana. Dall'antimoda allo stilismo*, edited by Grazietta Butazzi and Alessandra Mottola Molfino. Milan: Electa, 1987, pp. 288-95.